The Elements of Reasoning

The Elements of Reasoning

Second Edition

Edward P. J. Corbett

Late, The Ohio State University

Rosa A. Eberly

The University of Texas at Austin

Allyn and Bacon

Boston   London   Toronto   Sydney   Tokyo   Singapore

Vice President: Eben W. Ludlow
Series Editorial Assistant: Grace Trudo
Executive Marketing Manager: Lisa Kimball
Editorial-Production Service: Susan Freese, Communicáto, Ltd.
Text Design and Electronic Composition: Denise Hoffman
Composition Buyer: Linda Cox
Manufacturing Buyer: Suzanne Lareau
Cover Administrator: Jenny Hart

Library of Congress Cataloging-in-Publication Data

Corbett, Edward P. J.
    The elements of reasoning / Edward P. J. Corbett,
Rosa A. Eberly — 2nd ed.
      p.   cm. — (The elements of composition series)
    Includes index.
    ISBN 0-205-31511-9
    1. Reasoning. 2. Critical thinking. I. Eberly, Rosa A.
II. Title. III. Series.
BC177.C68   2000   00-026637
160–dc21   CIP

*See permissions credits on pages 145–146, which constitute a continuation
of the copyright page.*

Printed in the United States of America

10 9 8 7 6 5 4 3 2 1   05 04 03 02 01 00

For Once, Then, Something

*Others taunt me with having knelt at well-curbs
Always wrong to the light, so never seeing
Deeper down in the well than where the water
Gives me back in a shining surface picture
Me myself in the summer heaven godlike
Looking out of a wreath of fern and cloud puffs.
Once, when trying with chin against a well-curb,
I discerned, as I thought, beyond the picture,
Through the picture, a something white, uncertain,
Something more of the depths—and then I lost it.
Water came to rebuke the too clear water.
One drop fell from a fern, and lo, a ripple
Shook whatever it was lay there at bottom,
Blurred it, blotted it out. What was that whiteness?
Truth? A pebble of quartz? For once, then, something.*

—Robert Frost

Contents

Preface

This second edition of *The Elements of Reasoning* is intended to acquaint a wide readership with the elemental places, paths, and structures of reasoning and argumentation. It is not that I presume you are unfamiliar with argumentation; whether conscious of it or not, we are all surrounded by argumentation every hour of every day, and we engage in reasoning with ourselves and with others pretty much continually. This book offers an introduction to reasoning as well as time-tested tools for analyzing and producing your own arguments. By becoming acquainted with the many ways human beings can reason through language, we can become better reasoners ourselves and be put on guard against those who might try to deceive us.

The late Edward P. J. Corbett—who wrote the first edition of this book along with many other books on rhetoric, rhetoric and poetics, and written language—gave his blessing to my ideas for revising this edition several months before he passed away in June 1998. In this edition, I echo his comments from the preface of the first edition:

> What will be presented here, in a very succinct form, will be the basic strategies of argumentation that were first formulated by the ancient Greeks in their arts of rhetoric and dialectic. The ancient Greeks merely codified the processes that human beings engaged in from the beginning of time. . . . What philosophers like Plato and Isocrates and Aristotle did was observe how people argued with one another and then formulate theories and principles that would guide the practice of others who wanted to become effective arguers.

What I have augmented in this edition of *The Elements of Reasoning* are the Isocratean and Ciceronean traditions of reasoning. In addition, I have used some twentieth-century work—most notably that of Chaim Perelman and Lucie Olbrechts-Tyteca, Kenneth Burke, and Father W. A.

Grimaldi—to emphasize that reason and argumentation are as much about identification and agreement as they are about division. Moreover, reason does not mean mere rationality removed from the emotional response of reasoning partners (what Aristotle called *pathos*) or the character of the speaker or writer (what Aristotle called *ethos*). I have also changed the structure of the book to reflect not the modes of discourse but the *stasis questions,* as is reflected in the titles of Chapters 3 through 7. This book also has been influenced by the work of Frederick Antczak, Wayne Booth, Sharon Crowley, Lisa Ede, Jeanne Fahnestock, Gerard Hauser, Kathleen Hall Jamieson, Henry Johnstone, David Kaufer, James Kinneavy, Richard Lanham, Andrea Lunsford, Michael Leff, Robert McChesney, Richard McKeon, Marie Secor, and Stephen Toulmin.

Finally, I have emphasized the practice of reasoning together through language as an alternative to violence. This book has rhetoric at its core and active citizenship as its end. Thus, I have added a final chapter, Becoming a Citizen Critic, which encourages the practice of active public reasoning as a means of reinvigorating our democracy—from both within and outside colleges and universities.

While this book fits well into undergraduate college courses on rhetoric and composition or argument, or on speech, or on moral philosophy, it is also intended for courses across the curriculum and for people outside educational institutions. My examples focus on public issues of local, national, and international concern, and I encourage instructors and other users of this book to find examples of local public discourse to illustrate the elements of reasoning as discussed herein. While students of particular disciplines will be able to bring the special topoi of their fields to bear on these questions, general interest readers will have a great deal to bring to the book, as well. The examples are meant to engage a wide range of readers in reasoned contemplation and conversation about issues of common concern.

Preparing this edition of *The Elements of Reasoning* after Professor Corbett's death was a particularly humbling experience. As has been remarked elsewhere and by many, the prominence of rhetoric and composition in English studies is due in no small part to the indefatigable efforts of Professor Corbett and his many students.

Although I have retained several of Professor Corbett's examples from the first edition, the *I* in this second edition is me alone. As Professor Corbett said in the first edition:

> Succinct as this book is, it may tell you more about the basic strategies of argument than you care to know. Nevertheless, if you absorb these lessons well, you could be equipped for life with some skills that may prove to be very valuable as a citizen of the world.

Indeed, *The Elements of Reasoning* introduces you to an ancient but vitally contemporary practice that can help you become a participant, rather than merely a spectator, in many kinds of reasoning about issues of common concern.

Acknowledgments

I am grateful, first and foremost, to Edward P. J. Corbett and his first edition of this book, which I used during my first several years as a Professor of Rhetoric at The University of Texas at Austin. The book was particularly useful in my course on The University of Texas tower shootings and public memory.

Words of thanks also are due my colleagues in the Division of Rhetoric and Composition, the Department of Speech Communication, the Department of English, and the Department of Classics at The University of Texas at Austin and, more generally, the generous and inventive community of teachers and scholars in rhetoric, composition, and communication across the United States, whose conversation and company have enriched my ideas. Eben Ludlow and Doug Day of Allyn and Bacon and series editor William A. Covino have encouraged me to follow my intuitions, and for their enthusiasms I am also grateful.

Writing this book would not have been possible without the support of my family—particularly, Dick and Connie Diehl and their son Keith. My siblings—Sarah Kessler, Austin Eberly II, and Martha Gordon—my elders all, are ultimately responsible for my interest in reasoning.

Finally, the generous spirit and careful readings of Dr. Gina Siesing of The University of Texas at Austin and Harvard University, who reviewed this book for Allyn and Bacon and made copious comments on early drafts of each chapter, have been an enormous help and encouragement to me.

R. A. E.

1

Reasoning

Are You For It or Against It?

The Powers of Reasoning

Reasoning, by itself, will not get the potatoes peeled. Reasoning alone cannot sail a boat—or even keep it afloat. Reasoning cannot make flowers grow or get the really tough stains out. Reasoning, in and of itself, cannot get you back into your favorite jeans from tenth grade. Reasoning, like all other human things, has its limits. It cannot allow us to know the future in all its particulars.

For human beings, however, the ability to reason, using language in groups as well as by ourselves, remains our best hope for getting along—with ourselves and with each other. This book, an introduction to practical reasoning, endeavors to help you learn to practice reasoning by yourself and with others so that you can accomplish a universe of other things.

Reasoning is not arm twisting. It does not always result in making a sale. Reasoning rarely happens during shouting matches or on television talk shows. Reasoning is not a matter of winning or losing, of pressing 1 for *Yes* or 2 for *No.* Reasoning does not merely ask: Are you for it or against it? Reasoning is more nuanced and important than contemporary American culture seems to realize. Reasoning is, most importantly, not about certainty. Reasoning is as much about agreement as conflict, cooperation as discord, identification as division. Reasoning is a productive alternative to violence.

Why do you need to learn about reasoning? Reasoning in language—or *arguing,* as it is more commonly known today—is a uniquely human activity. It is distinct from physical force as a means of processing and resolving differences between and among individuals and groups. Reasoning is also a means by which individuals figure things out for themselves and with others. So reasoning is the basic practice of thinking human beings. You cannot escape the need for reasoning in any facet of your daily life: work, school, contemplation, relationships, citizenship. This book aims at teaching you how to reason more soundly, more reflectively, more effectively.

The kind of arguing we will discuss in this book will not always involve some sort of contest or contention involving two or more persons. Sometimes reasoning seeks only to persuade someone to accept an idea or to adopt a certain course of action—or simply to change the *reasoner's* own mind about something. Arguing can be done in a friendly way. Indeed, for some people, reasoning through language can be a source of pleasure or even recreation.

This chapter articulates the problem that this small but potentially powerful book sets out to solve: Most people hold definitions of *reasoning, argument,* and *rhetoric* that are not helpful to their being able to produce practical arguments. Whether the ideas in this book become powerful depends on you—on what you do with what you have learned after you put the book away.

Elemental Questions

What are the elements of reasoning? And what kind of question, do you think, is *that?*

These two questions are the keys to unlocking the powerful subject of this book. So let's reason them through.

First, the latter question. What kind of question is *What are the elements of reasoning?* Well, to begin, what is an element? An *element* is a fundamental or essential or irreducible part. Any statement that asks a question or makes a claim about the elements of something is definitional. At the same time, it makes a kind of claim about quality. Elements are essential, rather than optional, parts. How to begin to distinguish claims of quality from claims of definition is one of the many things we will examine in this book, and we will begin that process at the end of this chapter.

Knowing what kind of statement you are trying to make or what kind of question you are trying to ask—or someone else is asking of you—is a big help in reasoning. Why? Each kind of question, or **stasis,** brings with it a specific set of processes and structures. We will return to this concept later in this chapter. And throughout this book, we will focus on several additional central concepts in practical reasoning, many of which have been around for roughly 2,500 years. These concepts—**induction, deduction, example, enthymeme, ethos, pathos,** and **logos**—constitute the specific elements of reasoning in language, along with **topoi,** a powerful concept that delimits areas or regions of invention. Again, we will discuss these specific rhetorical concepts in detail in this chapter and the next, and we will use them throughout the book.

Now, back to the first question: *What are the elements of reasoning?* Language and human beings are the necessary elements of reasoning. Human beings, alone or in pairs or in groups, exercise their reasoning through language. *The Elements of Reasoning* will provide you with fundamental rhetorical concepts to identify kinds of questions and, just as important, to figure out how to begin inventing your answers by reasoning with yourself and with others.

Pluto and Plato

In January 1999, news arrived that Pluto was not, after all, a planet. How could that be? Every schoolchild since the mid-1930s has learned that our solar system comprises nine planets—and that the ninth is Pluto. What else could Pluto be, if not a planet?

The astronomer who started the controversy argued that, based on its size and mass, Pluto should be a minor planet, or asteroid, and thus be called *Minor Planet No. 10,000.* Another suggested that Pluto be designated a *Trans-Neptunian Object*—an object in the outer solar system whose distance from the sun is greater than that of Neptune and that is not a comet. Something that had been assumed to be a fact—an object of certainty, rather than an object of reasoning or argument—was now being argued about not just by astronomers but by various publics. An article about the controversy even appeared in *Parade*, a weekend newspaper insert read by roughly 82 million people weekly. David Levy, writing for *Parade* (May 30, 1999), said that "the controversy is about more than semantics. It relates to how 'we the people' view science and scientists." The *Parade* article opened to a wide audience the question of whose authority settles issues of fact and definition.

As public discussion about Pluto widened, the history of Pluto itself became the object of publicity. As reported in the *Washington Post* (March 10, 1999):

> When Clyde Tombaugh, a Kansas farm boy and would-be astronomer, arrived at Lowell Observatory in January 1929 to join the search for a planet beyond Neptune, a very experienced astronomer took him aside and warned that he would be wasting his time.
>
> Within a year after he began looking, however, Tombaugh had discovered Pluto. Tombaugh was too poor to attend college, but his name and Pluto's soon were in all the textbooks.

Pluto, it seems, has been a problem for experts all along. Other news reports have suggested that astronomers present at the time of Pluto's discovery did not agree on whether it was a planet or not. As reported in *Sky & Telescope* magazine (May 1, 1999), the International Astronomical Union (IAU) did not denominate Pluto as a planet after its discovery; neither did the American Astronomical Society or Britain's Royal Astronomical Society.

So how did we all learn that Pluto is a planet? As explained in *Sky & Telescope:*

> Despite some early suspicion that the newfound object was a giant comet with a parabolic orbit or an asteroid associated with Neptune, the fact that Pluto had been tracked down during Lowell Observatory's dedicated search for a trans-Neptunian planet held sway with astronomical opinion.

In other words, astronomers publicized Pluto as a planet because they had been looking for a planet. As *Sky & Telescope* concluded:

> Influenced then, as now, by public opinion, the astronomical community accepted the new object as a planet of full rank within a very few months.

The public was so interested in news about the new planet that Walt Disney, also taken with the story of the discovery of Pluto, named his cartoon dog after the orb.

Arguments about Pluto's planetary status suggest that even scientific definitions are the result of human reasoning through language. Writing in the *Washington Post* (March 10, 1999), Stephen P. Maran, assistant director of space sciences for information and outreach at NASA's Goddard Space Flight Center, made this very clear:

> The episode in which Pluto's planethood has been challenged but reaffirmed reminds us that, if scientists have difficulty agreeing on their terms, others can be excused for similar uncertainty. In fact, astronomers have changed their definitions of "planet" over the years.
>
> To the ancients, planets were the bright "stars" that did not stay in their constellations but roamed across the sky. "Planet" itself is derived from the Greek word for "wanderer." We know now that planets are not stars, but learning that took time.
>
> So a planet is a round object orbiting directly around the sun that shines by reflected light and is larger than the known asteroids and that may have an atmosphere.
>
> We can go with that definition, or we can accept that, above all, Pluto is a planet because people have called it a planet for 70 years and like it that way.

Indeed, *tradition* was consistently cited as the central reason for retaining Pluto's status as a planet after the IAU declared later in 1999 that Pluto, for the time being, would remain our ninth planet.

Before the IAU ruling on Pluto, however, experts were arguing—reasoning together through language—about which definition of a planet is best and whether Pluto conforms to that definition. Nonexperts, however, were also talking and writing—reasoning together—about the question. Some people even wrote letters to the editor to try to influence others' opinions about what many people would consider a question of fact—whether a planet is a planet. The Pluto story broke just before the U.S. Senate's impeachment trial of President Clinton began. In a way that suggests how language precedes and as such is an element of reasoning, one writer suggested that the ninth planet was "being impeached." And in another letter to the editor, this one from the *Boston Globe* (January 23, 1999), Ian Vogt of Portsmouth, New Hampshire, wrote:

> Poor, sweet little Pluto is tucked away in a far corner of the solar system, minding its own business. Now, astronomers want to play with its planet status just because it is small and has an eccentric orbit. Being "Trans-Neptunian Object No. 1" is small consolation.
>
> If they get away with this, what will be next? Will they look at Mercury and say, "No real planet should be so close to the Sun"? Hello, "Trans-Venusian Object No. 1"!
>
> Will they look at Jupiter and say, "It doesn't really have a surface"? Will they look at Venus and say, "We already have a planet just like it"? Soon, there will be only two planets: Earth and Mars. Mars will be kept around so we have another planet to feel superior to, our planetary side-kick.
>
> I think astronomers should go back to pondering the really big questions of life, the universe, and everything.

Vogt reasons through language by personifying Pluto, by using emotional appeals (or pathos), and by employing a strategy sometimes known as a *slippery slope* argument. Combined, all these means of reasoning together in language suggest that, for Vogt at least, astronomers should ponder larger questions than whether a far-off planet—or even a nearer one, including our own—conforms to an abstract definition. Vogt's letter also reminds us that reasoning is not all about formal logic; again, human beings reason by various means, a point we will return to presently.

The history of reasoning about Pluto's status as a planet serves as a reminder that few things, even everyday facts, can be known for certain. It is precisely because of this lack of certainty that human reasoning through language emerged and became central to all human activities.

But if few things are certain, how do we make individual and collective judgments about that which could be otherwise?

Students in my rhetoric classes often feel intimidated to send out their arguments to newspapers, magazines, and local radio talk shows because, they say, they are not certain about everything they want to argue. Yet even most Nobel Prize–winning scientists know that the work they do neither proceeds from nor results in certainty. Rather, scientific research, like all human reasoning, is a process located in and limited by time and space.

"Being certain is not what science is about," explained Allison Richards on the National Public Radio (NPR) program *All Things Considered.* "One week, the universe is expanding; the next it is shrinking." Richards and the scientists she interviewed for her report stressed that scientific reasoning is a work in progress and that scientific papers represent researchers' best judgments at the time, using the best tools and the best evidence available.

If human reasoning concerned questions of certainty, computer programmers would have known to create date coding with more than two digits in the final slot. Imagine a world in which no one would had to have heard (or worried) about Y2K glitches!

This rhetorical view of reasoning is very different from how scientific research and knowledge are usually represented and understood. Since René Descartes declared in the seventeenth century that any human difference of opinion signified an error by one party or another, science and logic have seen as necessarily false those things that are only possible or probable. Arguably, this view of knowledge as certainty can be traced back 2,500 years to Plato, who distrusted human opinion because of its changing nature. For Plato, true knowledge was unarguable and definitions were absolute and unchanging. What our Pluto example shows is that definitions themselves are the result of collective human reasoning through language—and that even the heavens do not admit to certainty, particularly from our earthly view.

Fine Language and Geometry

Plato's student Aristotle—who was concerned with human reasoning, rather than divine absolutes—observed that "you do not need fine language to speak about geometry." Geometry, at least the kind of geometry that Aristotle knew, involved computation, or counting and measuring, rather than reasoning, which involves language and human judgment. We need to make judgments only about things that are open to argument, things that can be otherwise. Doing geometry does not require reasoning, but discoursing about geometry does.

Unlike computation, rhetoric is concerned with all language, fine and not so fine. Because reasoning requires language, reasoning is unlike computation. Numbers allow us to measure energy coming from Pluto and to make other observations about it. But numbers alone will never determine whether Pluto is a planet. Such questions involve reasoning, and reasoning involves language.

So the elements of reasoning are language and human beings in relation with each other. And *rhetoric,* the art you will learn about and begin to practice by using and reusing this book, is the elemental art of humans and their language—written and spoken, read and heard.

In fact, as the letter writer who suggested Pluto was "being impeached" showed us, reasoning depends on language. How else can we deliberate but in words? The centrality of language to reasoning has been recognized by some in recent years in a way that it had not been since the Renaissance. This *rhetorical turn,* as it is sometimes called, suggests that we can learn a great deal about ourselves and our shared worlds by being mindful about the language we use to make our individual and collective judgments.

Chaim Perelman and Lucie Olbrechts-Tyteca, two twentieth-century Belgian scholars, argued that language has the force of *quasi-logical arguments.* In other words, the language through which we reason about things has the same force or effect as logic. The Latin word for figured language, *ornatus,* is a translation of the Greek *kosmos,* which means "world." Both suggest that to use language is to build a world, however limited by our humanness and however ephemeral.

The widely different reactions people had to the 1999 impeachment trial of President Clinton again serve as a touchstone for thinking about how world-making language functions in and precedes reasoning, particularly when people from different backgrounds are trying to reason together. "The Senate trial of President Clinton—and the issues that led to his impeachment—sparked strong opinions about truth, law, and morality," reported NPR's Linda Wertheimer (January 28, 1999). "But many people—politicians and citizens alike—disagree about the implications and importance of the president's actions."

NPR reporter Margot Adler interviewed Jerome Kagan, professor of psychology at Harvard University, who said that the following sentences offer insights into how language operates in reasoning:

The grandmother loves her granddaughter.

The lover loves her lover.

The wife loves her husband.

"In those three sentences," Kagan continued, "the word *love* has totally different meanings. But in the West we like the simple, naked predicate *love,* as if it means the same thing independent of the social context." The reporter continued:

> Kagan argues that when it comes to questions of law, the West tends to be similarly single-minded. The law is the law. "We don't care who the victims were—whether they were relatives or not or strangers or not; a felony is a felony. But in the East, that was never the case. It made a big difference whether one stole from a relative, a parent, a child. Those were very different situations. And I think what we're having here currently in the U.S., whereas in the past the law was Western and abstract, now, because of the heterogeneity in our population with respect to ethnic background and values, many Americans are coming to move more toward the Eastern view."

What the professor refers to as "the Eastern view" has a great deal in common with the rhetorical turn. The law is not the law is not the law, and a crime is not a crime is not a crime. The point, again, is that the definitions of law and crime—and beauty and justice and right and wrong—are all the products, however ephemeral, of human reasoning. Thus, they change and are subject to human judgment.

Do you recall Representative Henry Hyde calling the Senate "Mount Olympus" during the House hearings on impeachment? Hyde's world-building use of language suggested that it is in the Senate, not the House, where definitions such as what constitutes an impeachable offense are debated and judged. (Mount Olympus, of course, is the home of the gods in Greek mythology.) This view of language as central to reasoning is reminiscent of a statement by Isocrates, a rival of Plato and Aristotle.

Isocrates opened his most widely known treatise, *Against the Sophists,* by pointing out that sometimes even the gods argue with each other. So, he asks, how can mere mortals deceive themselves by thinking they can know absolutes? The best option we have—particularly as a productive alternative to violence—is to reason together through language.

Ethos, Logos, and Pathos

Sir Philip Sidney complained as early as the sixteenth century about the split 'twixt the tongue and the heart—and he was certainly not the first to do so. Because reasoning is a practice conducted through language, it is an embodied practice, or one carried on by deliberating bodies—individually, in pairs and in groups, in institutions and outside them. Thus, those who want to reason are not helped by a definition of reasoning—or a history of philosophy or rhetoric—that stresses only its rational or cerebral elements. Reasoning is too often understood as merely logos, and logos is too often reduced to logic or Cartesian rationality. I follow Father William M. A. Grimaldi in seeing ethos, logos, and pathos as the means of persuasion and all of them as operating through enthymemes and examples.

So what are ethos, logos, and pathos? And why do you need to know these smelly old Greek words to practice reasoning?

Well, of course, you don't need the Greek words to reason. However, the Greek distinctions among these three kinds of persuasion are helpful shorthand ways to remember complex concepts.

First, there is **ethos.** The closest English word we have to ethos in meaning is *character;* however, character means only a part of what ethos signified to the Greeks.

For Aristotle, in particular, ethos was part of the art of rhetoric. That is to say, the self the *rhetor*—that is, the speaker or writer—presented to the assembly or in the marketplace was a constructed self, a mindful self, a public self—a self that did not necessarily equate with the person inside or the authentic self, which was unknowable. Thinking about the self you present in face-to-face, group, or written reasoning as a means of persuasion—or just as importantly, thinking about how different kinds of selves persuade you—is a fundamentally important element of reasoning. Again, there is nothing irrational about how ethos works; in fact, Aristotle's *Rhetoric* is largely a catalog of how different kinds of selves persuade and can be persuaded. Reasoning always operates, at least in part, through the ethos of the speaker or writer.

Although it sounds like *logic,* the meaning of **logos** is much richer than the connotations of dry logic. Logos is reasoning as it is embodied in a text, whether written or spoken. Logos is the text of reasoning itself apart from the character of the speaker or the emotional response of the hearer or reader.

Finally, **pathos** is the emotional impact of reasoning or argument on the listener or reader. As he did with ethos, Aristotle listed premises for judging which arguments would affect which kinds of audiences through pathos.

All three appeals—ethos, logos, and pathos—are rational. Ethos and pathos are neither irrational nor arational; they simply have rationalities of their own. It is where each is focused—ethos in the rhetor, logos in the text itself, and pathos in the listener or hearer—that distinguishes them.

The End of Reasoning

The end (as in the goal or the destination) of reasoning is **judgment,** but you will not always be able to get there. What do I mean by *judgment?* First, I do not mean ultimate or final judgment. Again, because we are humans limited by space and time, we cannot know in an absolute or final sense. What I mean by judgment is, following Aristotle's language, **krisis:** a point at which a decision must be made—as well as the particular decision that is made. Sometimes, however, you may leave the processes and structures of reasoning without being able to come to a judgment, for one reason or another. Then, your judgment might be: "I can't yet make a judgment on that. Perhaps I'll get back to it."

To understand the idea of krisis as occurring at *a point* in time, we should review two different ways of thinking about time, which had distinct words in ancient Greek. The first, **kronos,** which persists in modern English in the word *chronology,* signifies the kind of time that has a beginning, middle, and end. Chronological time is time passing. Think of it as a number line with arrows at both ends. The other kind of time, **kairos,** has no direct equivalent in English, yet it is still a powerful concept for thinking about reasoning and judgment. Kairos signifies the right moment or the opportune moment. Think of it as a point on the number line. In chronological time, particular moments arise that clearly call for judgment—hence the connection between *kairos,* the opportune moment, and *krisis,* or judgment.

Individually or as part of a group, you may decide that you do not have enough information or the right people to make a decision; even that is a judgment. Shared judgment constitutes human beings' best hope for having a sound basis from which to act reasonably and mindfully.

Judgment, however, can take more than one form. For instance, it can take the form of understanding—critical reading and listening. This process takes place through a dialogue you can learn to develop within yourself. Imagine that you see a bright blue bird in a park near where you live. Knowing something about birds, you wonder whether the bird is an eastern bluebird or an indigo bunting. You might have to reason with yourself through internal language about how to identify the particular bird:

What size is the bird?

What is the date?

What is the bird doing?

Is the bird all blue, or is it marked with brown?

Answering these questions will help you figure out what kind of bird the visitor might be.

We will call this first form of judgment **internal.** Reading this book and practicing the concepts you find here will help you become a better listener, a more careful and critical reader, and a better reasoner about all kinds of texts—from letters to the editor to creatures in your environment. In turn, practicing internal reasoning will help you have more confidence in the judgments you come to when you reason by yourself. Do not mistake internal reasoning for reasoning in a vacuum. Contrary to Descartes's famous *cogito ergo sum,* we can never reason unaffected by the discourses and influences of others.

Judgment has another form, as well. In addition to internal reception and understanding, reasoning is an important element of producing discourses **external** to the self, written and spoken, individual and communal. In fact, to reason through language and produce discourses by yourself and with others is a central means by which human beings can come to terms with or perhaps change their circumstances (a topic we will return to in Chapters 7 and 8). Imagine again that you have seen and identified that blue bird. You have decided that it is an indigo bunting and that other people need to know and care that indigo buntings are visiting your area. So you write a letter to the editor of your weekly community newspaper or call the local talk radio show during the Saturday morning gardening hour to make people aware that indigo buntings are nesting in your neighborhood.

This kind of reasoning also involves dialogue, but in this case, the dialogue is between more than just a listener or reader and a text. This second kind of judgment—external—is explicitly collaborative and directed to someone outside yourself. Both ends concern judgment, and that is the ultimate end of reasoning. Besides helping you reason through questions internally, this book will help you become a better external reasoner and encourage you to share the fruits of your reasoning and judgments with others.

Internal and External Reasoning: An Example

The following extended—and, frankly, very troubling—example will help clarify that the end of reasoning is judgment and that the forms of reasoning and judgment are internal and external.

In late February 1999, John William King of Jasper, Texas, was found guilty of, to quote the *Washington Post* (February 26, 1999), "the racial murder of James Byrd Jr., a black man who was chained to a pickup truck in the predawn darkness and dragged on a winding stretch of pavement until his head and right arm were torn off." The gruesome murder left many in Texas and the nation reasoning together about the kind of world they lived in, a shared world that would create and foster such hateful violence.

The day after the verdict, people began to reason together about media coverage of the trial. Two listener responses to news coverage on NPR suggest that reasoning is more complicated than asking: Are you for it or against it? In addition, these responses suggest that reasoning can be understood as a dialogue between a text—in this case, the news coverage on NPR—and individual listeners. Here are transcripts of the responses, broadcast from taped messages left in the respondents' own voices (February 26, 1999):

Transcript 1

Hi. This is Sandy Smith. And I live in Jefferson, Oregon. I would just like to tell you that I am quite appalled by the gruesome details that have been thrown at us as listeners about Byrd. There is just so much sensationalism in the news, and I don't need to hear it all. I don't mind you telling me briefly how he was killed, but I don't think that the gory details are necessary.

Transcript 2

This is Peggy Safire in New Fairfield, Connecticut. I want to say that I hope you never flinch from exposing the homicidal underbelly of racists. Every one of us ought to be brought to tears and anguish as we imagine the nightmare Mr. Byrd was left to endure at the hands of these racists. This is the least we can do as mere listeners and spectators. By bearing witness to the truths of what hate and haters do, as we do by hearing NPR's report, we can honor the life of this innocent so brutally taken.

At first hearing—or reading—these two people seem to agree on very little. Yet each is making a potentially reasonable argument: the first that some news is too sensational to be broadcast, no matter how important, and the second that the deeds were so heinous and odious, so hateful, that the details must be widely broadcast. Just being able to hear what people are arguing—and that their arguments show agreement as well as disagreement—is a big step toward becoming a better reasoner.

What is the precise issue they disagree on? The quality or value of NPR broadcasting the gruesome details of James Byrd's death. What do they agree on? First, that the details of the broadcast were, indeed, graphic. Second, that the question of what upsetting details should be broadcast is an important one. And third, that if they share their discourses with NPR and with other listeners, they will be heard and perhaps their arguments will influence NPR policies—and quite possibly the opinions of other listeners. Overall, Smith's and Safire's arguments manifest a shared faith in the power of reasoning.

As I listened to these rhetors on my portable radio headphones, walking my dogs, I started thinking about the issues they raised. I turned off the radio and kept walking, reasoning internally about the responsibilities of various news media to report the details of crimes. Because I previously had worked as a newspaper reporter and editor, I recalled situations where other editors and I had discussed whether to publish details of certain crimes—a particularly exigent question when crimes are still under investigation. In other words, I used the discourses of the two active listeners in combination with my prior experiences to begin forming my own reasoned judgment of NPR's coverage of the King verdict.

If you had heard Smith's and Safire's arguments that day, perhaps you would have begun to form a judgment of the NPR coverage of the trial by reasoning through internal language. What is *sensationalism?* How much description is too much? By what criteria should you or should a society judge such questions? Is violent news coverage different from the presentation of other kinds of violence in the media? How is violence portrayed or communicated differently via radio than via television or print or the World Wide Web?

The questions that you might have invented from listening to Smith and Safire are literally infinite. This is *internal* reasoning, and it is vital to the quality of our individual and shared lives. Again, understanding others' arguments in order to find points of identification is the best alternative we have for getting along with others.

This kind of reader or listener forum is about as close to public discourse as Americans get anymore. Radio and television talk shows are designed to titillate viewers and sell advertising, not to initiate reasoned discussion about issues of common concern. Some shows—such as one that tracks down unfaithful partners and captures them on videotape— are designed to incite violence. Such shows turn viewers into voyeurs, rather than participants in caring, reasoned discussion. Radio and television networks, along with magazines and newspapers, target specific demographic groups so that different kinds of people do not have to read about what is beyond their narrow interests—much less interact with each other. And beyond the media, few public spaces exist anymore where we can see each other and get a sense of our power as a people— much less reason with each other in public. Although there are currently relatively few venues in which to engage in truly public discourse, learning to be a careful listener and to engage in internal reasoning is one means of participating in what opportunities do exist for reasoning about questions of common concern.

Despite their strong differences of opinion, Smith and Safire were reasoning together about the fate of their common world—and their common radio program. They are both also clearly concerned for the world in which such a crime could occur—their shared world. Their responses show that all argument begins in identification or agreement of some kind—otherwise, there would be no conversation, dialogue, or reasoning going on at all.

If listening to Smith's and Safire's responses elicited a strong reaction in you, you might want to participate in the conversation that their voice mail responses started. This would involve the second form of reasoning, *external* reasoning. Perhaps you might want to try to contact one of them by writing a letter or sending an e-mail. Perhaps you may want to write about the issues raised by Smith and Safire in another medium. Perhaps you will find yourself returning—through memory—several times during the next few days to a particular issue raised by their interchange; you might want to reason through language with a trusted friend or two about what they think of the issues Smith and Safire argued about. Through external reasoning, you can form sounder judgments by collaborating with others. And you can share the conclusions you reach, however provisionally, with others through language.

Rhetorical Inventions: Beyond "For or Against"

Smith's and Safire's responses show how the discourses of others can be inventional for your own reasoning. What do I mean by *inventional?* Invention is one of the five *canons,* or bodies of knowledge, of *rhetoric,* the art of practical reasoning. To say that something is inventional, or that it prompts invention, is to say that it is thought provoking—at least to someone who has learned to practice reasoning by learning elemental concepts of rhetoric!

Why do you need rhetoric? If you have an idea, need an idea, or want to know what to make of an idea, you need rhetoric. If you learn and practice rhetoric, you can invent things to say and work toward having a practiced judgment of what to say and what not to say. This book attempts to acquaint interested readers with understanding and using the powerful art of rhetoric through practicing the elements of reasoning.

Here is an example of the power of invention: I once asked my spouse what it is like to live with a rhetorician. Taking his characteristically measured time to respond, he said, "Words escape me."

Students come to my rhetoric classes already persuaded by the confrontational discourses they too often hear around them that reasoning is nothing more than being for or against something. One of the strengths of the vocabulary of rhetoric is that it allows us to describe with more precision the kinds of arguments that others are making—and those that we wish to make. Learning the elemental vocabulary of rhetoric and practicing it by reasoning through language is what this book is about.

For instance, that Smith and Safire disagree on the **stasis** of value or quality is important to notice. What do I mean by *stasis?* This is a fundamental rhetorical concept, one that—as shown by the table of contents—structures this entire book. I will go into more detail about stasis in the next chapter, but what follows is a brief introduction that will enable you to begin practicing.

Arguably inchoate and unnamed in Aristotle's treatise on rhetoric, the stasis questions were probably invented by Hermagoras of Temnos two centuries after Aristotle. The stasis questions, or stases, provide a relatively straightforward way of classifying claims. Given the amount and intensity of discourses that rush past us each day, having a means of quickly classifying those claims in order to be a better critical listener and reader is a huge help in becoming a better reasoner. Here are the five stases:

1. *Questions of conjecture*—for example, What happened? Does a shared reality exist?

2. *Questions of definition*—for example, What should we call it?

3. *Questions of cause and consequence*—for example, How did this come to happen? What will follow from it?

4. *Questions of value*—for example, Is this good or bad? Is this functional? Is this just?

5. *Questions of procedure and proposal*—for example, What should we do about this?

Any claim can be understood as one of these types of questions. Again, we will discuss these further in Chapter 2 and throughout the book, but for now, commit them to memory and get ready to use them for practice at the end of this chapter.

In this chapter, I have endeavored to reason with you through language about why reasoning is so important to you and to our public culture and about how knowing rhetorical concepts—the stasis questions, in particular—can help you be a better reasoner, both internally and externally. The next chapter will continue our discussion of the stasis questions and introduce other particular elements of reasoning—topoi, induction, deduction, enthymeme, and example. Chapters 3 through 7 will introduce you to the processes and structures of each stasis question, one at a time. Finally, Chapter 8, Becoming a Citizen Critic, will encourage you to practice rhetoric actively and to share your reasoned judgments with others.

Before we move on to the next chapter, however, you need to begin your own practice of reasoning. Reasoning is a practice. Like playing the piano or doing tai chi, reasoning is manifest in its practice. This book will help you learn and habituate the practice of reasoning through the ancient and venerable art of rhetoric. Following are three examples of reasoning for you to read. As you read—and I suggest that you begin to read aloud discourses that you want to study—keep the introduction to stasis in mind, and begin now to practice using the elements of reasoning.

❖ *Reasoning Practice*

Read the following examples of practical reasoning, and for each consider the following four questions:

- How might this prompt internal reasoning?
- How might this prompt external reasoning?
- What are the central claims?
- How might you respond to one of these claims?

1. From a column by Jon Carroll in the *San Francisco Chronicle* (July 22, 1999).

Death by Drowning
Jon Carroll
There are various stages of mourning, or so I am given to understand, and I am at the anger stage, so y'all may have to forgive me.

First: A few months ago I wrote about my dear friend Alexander McIntire, who had disappeared in Miami under mysterious circumstances. I had hoped then—believed then, I now realize—that he was somehow still alive, on the run from personal demons or lost in a strange amnesiac state.

Alex's body was discovered late Monday inside his van submerged in a canal near the Everglades. He loved the peace and privacy of the Everglades; he took me there when I visited him; he would go there sometimes to meditate and take photographs.

He died of drowning. His body had been in the water a long time. There are no other useful facts. I am flying to Miami over the weekend for the memorial service.

Alex was a wonderful friend, a gentle voice on the telephone, a scholar, a loving father, a man who constantly sought to take comfort in faith, the evidence of things unseen.

And may I add: Damn damn damn damn damn damn damn. I shall also add stronger words. As a mutual friend said: There are very few people in the world whom I admire; now there is one less. God damn it anyway. Oh, Alex.

I had thought to write something about the death of John F. Kennedy Jr., but then I got the news about Alex and somehow writing about the death by drowning of a celebrity seemed a little much. It still seems a little much. Nevertheless.

I have no opinions about John F. Kennedy as a human being. I did not know him. I felt no twinge of anything when I heard about his plane, except for the vague universal sadness I feel every morning when I read the obituary page.

But I have opinions about the news coverage, about three networks staying on the air all day long showing enlightening photographs of blank patches of ocean while experts talked about the handling capabilities of aircraft and the curse of the Kennedys and the Coast Guard procedures and anything else they could think of, just filling airtime, until everyone got so sloppy that, reportedly, Dan Rather found himself reciting the lyrics to "Camelot"—a show tune, for heaven's sake—and then choking up on air.

And why were they on the air? The real dirty reason was that none of the networks wanted any of the other networks to beat them to the money shot, the corpse floating in the water or even the poignant purse bobbing on the waves. They didn't want to be in regular programming while the image the world would remember was flashed on other networks.

So they wallowed. There was no news. They wallowed. I have never hated the cult of celebrity more.

We all have real lives. We have mothers and sisters and sons and friends and teachers. We have people in pain around us, people who need us, people who will one day not be around anymore. And yet Americans seem to spend their time fretting about the tragedies and triumphs of some semi-imaginary set of demigods.

Not now, honey, I'm watching the ocean that might be near the place where the plane of a person I never knew maybe crashed. I can't come to the phone, give you dinner, visit your house, hug you—John-John is missing!

Creating myths is an ancient recreation. Centralizing the myths using mediated environments is somewhat newer. The Kennedys have a right to privacy and a right to grieve. Your job is to turn off the TV and find a person you love and tell him so.

2. From *The Rush Limbaugh Program,* a nationally syndicated radio talk show (March 1999):

Not every environmentalist is a wacko. I do not believe, for example, that wanting clean air and clean water is the definition of an environmentalist today. We all want clean air and clean water. Everybody does. It's silly to have to go out and say you're for it because I can't find anybody who's against it.

3. Any paragraph or section from this chapter

2

Invention

Places, Paths, and Structures of Reasoning

An Introduction to the Specific Elements

Let's say you are taking a break from cleaning the grout in your shower, and you turn on the regional cable television network. What you see surprises you: a group of men in what looks to be a hand-carved canoe, a few more men in the water, a huge harpooned whale at the center of their attention, and the sea stained red as far as the camera spans.

What happened?

What should we call this?

What are its causes and consequences?

What values are associated with it?

What should we do about this?

The stasis questions provide points of entry to begin internal and external reasoning about, well, anything. Though they grew out of the discourses of the Hellenistic law courts, the stases are generalizable to any kind of reasoning and argumentation. They are a powerful tool, particularly when combined with the other rhetorical concepts you will learn in this chapter.

Chapter 1 argued that, given that human beings and language are the elements of reasoning, you are uniquely equipped to become a good reasoner by practicing reasoning by yourself and with others. This chapter will spell out how to do that by giving you several concepts to help you become a better internal and external reasoner. But first we have to talk about road trips. And invention.

As we discussed in Chapter 1, invention is one of the bodies of knowledge of rhetoric. Here are all of the bodies of knowledge, or *canons,* of rhetoric:

Invention—finding and making things to say or write

Arrangement—putting those things in order

Style—considering how you have said or written things

Memory—being able to recall things

Delivery—getting your inventions across to others

The canons of rhetoric are not unlike the stages in the writing process—prewriting, drafting, editing, an so on. But because rhetoric was first theorized as a verbal art of speaking, memory and delivery were also central parts of the art, though they have no direct equivalents in contemporary writing pedagogy. Memory and delivery, however, are still important to being able to reason well. In fact, no reasoning in thought, speech, or writing would be possible without memory. How can we reason about things if we cannot hold them in our minds?

Of the canons, this book focuses almost entirely on *invention*—finding and making things to say or write in the process of reasoning. When the book does touch on the other canons, it does so by focusing on how they augment invention.

Rhetoric offers several tools of invention to anyone who wants to become a better reasoner. Of those tools, the best with which to begin to practice reasoning are the **stases,** because they help you build roads or paths into unmapped territory. That is to say, they help you to think in ways you may never have considered, and they take you to places of reasoning you may never have been.

Ever taken a road trip? Ever just driven or biked or canoed without knowing where you were going? Ever gotten lost in the woods, traveling without a path? I hope you have not been lost for long. It can be terrifying—after the excitement wanes!

For many people who do not practice reasoning, it is easy to get lost when trying to think through questions and issues. The stases help you see or hear where points of agreement and disagreement may occur. (Remember our discussion of the listeners who called National Public Radio in Chapter 1? Remember what stasis they disagreed at?)

In addition, the stases help you think about the possible directions in which your own reasoning might proceed. Thus, the stases help you build roads—or paths, if you like your traveling to be less intrusive—to find a way through the wide prairies, the dense forests, and even the terra incognita of reasoning.

Places of Reasoning: Topoi

Combined with the stases, another rhetorical concept—**topoi**—helps you find places you want to stop when you are on certain roads of reasoning. *Topoi* is an ancient Greek word meaning "places." (*Topoi* is plural and *topos* is singular.) Topoi provide you with places from which to start reasoning. What do I mean by that?

Rhetorician Michael Leff describes topoi as "the atomic units of discourse," while also noting that every rhetorical theorist, ancient or modern, who has discussed topoi has done so not only using different specific categories but also employing different metaphors ("Topics of Rhetorical Invention," 1983). Chaim Perelman and Lucie Olbrechts-Tyteca used the Latin, rather than the Greek, word for "place"; their book *The New Rhetoric* (1969) uses six common **loci** and defines them, following Cicero, as "storehouses for arguments." I define *topoi* as bioregions of discourse—that is, places where discourse can be planted and where reasoning may grow. We can also think about topoi this way: Topoi are what we talk about when we talk about X.

So topoi are atoms, storehouses, bioregions. Topoi are places where the reasoner can stop, however briefly, and hang her hat. Thus, topoi function as memory aids as well as inventional prompts: It is much easier to remember the paths of your reasoning if you have certain mileposts to recall. There is another metaphorical definition of topoi, then: remarkable places on the roads of reasoning. Places. What we talk about—places we stop and then start again—when we reason about whatever it is we are reasoning about.

When my students want to discuss an issue as a class, the first thing we do is build a map of the topoi surrounding that issue. Sometimes students do this at their computers, sometimes I do it at the chalkboard, and sometimes we just talk and all take notes about the various topoi we are inventing.

On the day of the school shootings in Littleton, Colorado, for instance, students came to class wanting to talk about the issue. After we spent time learning what was happening—the event was still under way at the time—we began making an inventional map of topoi on the board so that we could keep track of our internal and external collaborative reasoning.

One student mentioned school violence as a topos. Another mentioned video games. Another mentioned popular music. Another mentioned black trench coats. Somebody mentioned prayer. Someone else mentioned the media. Another student mentioned gun ownership. Soon we had nearly 40 places to begin our reasoning—nearly 40 topoi—about the shootings in Littleton.

Although this invention exercise gave us many places to begin our reasoning, none of them made us feel better about the tragedy that was happening at the time. Yet that leads to more topoi: The pain of such tragedies and how to cope with the pain itself is another place to begin reasoning. Also, the fact that reasoning does not in itself lead to change is a good reminder that reasoning has its limits. Nonetheless, topoi are the places where reasoning can begin; topoi are aids to remembering the roads you have traveled in your reasoning, and topoi are places to stop a while and catch your breath during the process of reasoning. And, as we will discuss when we return to the stases, reasoning is what gets us to the point of asking: What can we do about this?

There are two kinds of topoi, specific and common. *Specific* topoi are specific to a discipline (like physics or politics), to a subject (the Littleton shootings or fruit tree growing or baseball or whaling), to a kind of discourse (such as legal or commemorative), or to a stasis (procedure arguments always have to deal with the topos of feasibility, for instance). *Common* topoi, on the other hand, are concerned with all subjects. The common topoi, as first theorized by Aristotle, include:

the greater and the lesser

past fact, present fact, future fact

the possible and the impossible

Here is an example of *the greater and the lesser* that came up in our discussion of Littleton:

The shootings at Columbine High School were the biggest and worst school shootings in recent history in the United States.

Past fact, present fact, and future fact refers to whether a thing did exist, does exist, or will exist; this topos is very closely related to the stasis of conjecture, which we will discuss at length in the next chapter. Many students invented an example of this topos in our class discussion of the Littleton shootings: Kids shooting kids in schools did not used to happen. And we certainly need to try to find a way to stop it.

Finally, *the possible and the impossible,* also related to conjecture, deals with what might be or might not be possible. As we discussed Littleton, we repeatedly wondered whether anything could be done to prevent future shootings—whether it is possible to stop such a dangerous and troubling trend. (Notice the definitional move there, *trend?* I hope you did.)

Perelman and Olbrechts-Tyteca offer six common topoi as starting points of discourse, but their choices are somewhat different than those picked by Aristotle. Here are their six common topoi:

quantity

quality

order

existence

essence

person

Clearly, some of these topoi overlap with Aristotle's three common topoi above. *Quantity* sounds a great deal like *the greater and the lesser; order* and *existence* seem to combine *past fact, present fact, future fact*. However, the most important thing to recognize is that common topoi attempt to classify arguments that are commonly made about issues of concern to all—that is, issues that do not fall into one specific subject area or another, issues that are of concern to the public or various publics. As you practice using these topoi, they will become more familiar and eventually very useful to you in discussing issues of common concern.

So *topoi*, again, allow you to see and reason and invent from particular places. And *stases* allow you to see possible and actual points of agreement and/or disagreement as well as help you think about in what directions you may want your reasoning to proceed. Together, stases and topoi help you reason by helping you make and use an inventional road map of many possible starting places and directions of reasoning in response to an issue, question, or problem.

In addition to places (topoi) and paths (stases), the other rhetorical concepts we will focus on in this chapter are structures: **induction, example, deduction,** and **enthymeme.** We will also discuss a variant of the enthymeme called the **Toulmin system** of reasoning. All of these concepts are means of reasoning more soundly, internally and externally.

Paths of Reasoning: The Stases

So, back to the grout in your shower—or whatever it was you were doing when you heard about the harpooning of that gray whale.

What happened?

A headline in the *Boston Globe* (May 18, 1999) the next day made a claim at the stasis of conjecture, as most headlines do:

Tribe reclaims its past with harpoon thrust.

That's a claim about what happened: *Tribe reclaims past.* Conjectural claims usually have active verbs, rather than linking verbs.

The Associated Press (AP) story under the headline made a conjectural claim, as well:

NEAH BAY, Wash.—Makah Indians in a hand-carved canoe, renewing an ancient tribal tradition, harpooned a gray whale yesterday for the first time in 70 years.

In fact, since journalists are taught to limit their claims to conjectural claims—"just the facts, ma'am"—the next paragraph of the AP story is full of conjectural claims, as well:

> A larger fishing boat joined the hunters and began slowly towing the carcass to Neah Bay, where the 2,000-member tribe declared a holiday. Later in the day, tribal members lined the shore by the hundreds as a string of Indian canoes towed the whale into the harbor.

Claims of conjecture endeavor to answer the question: *What happened?* Like any claim, they are always located at least partly in the perspective of the person who is making the claim. According to the claims of conjecture in the *Globe* headline and the AP story, what happened was pretty straightforward. But here are other claims of conjecture that I found in just one news story about the Makah whaling event—other claims about what happened:

> "They have killed an intelligent, beautiful animal—just blown it away with an antitank gun," said Paul Watson, leader of Sea Shepherd International, a conservation group. (*New York Times*, May 18, 1999)

> "We made history today," Ben Johnson, chairman of the tribe's whaling council, said this afternoon. "This is a great day for the Makah Nation." (*New York Times*, May 18, 1999)

> The successful kill "restores a missing link in our heritage," said Arnie Hunter, vice president of the whaling commission, who rode in the support boat this morning. (*New York Times*, May 18, 1999)

In just one newspaper article, three different claims of conjecture offer their speakers' views of stasis question number one: *What happened?*

Reasoning at the stasis of conjecture suggests that humans do not always agree on what constitutes a *fact*. Because we are limited by space and time—by our bodies and their locations and by what we can perceive—we have no omniscient perch from which to see the "real" facts.

As the whaling example shows so clearly, facts are among the most contentious and fraught kinds of claims externally. Internally, conjecture claims are often more straightforward: If you saw something with your eyes or heard it with your ears or felt it with your own sensing skin, you are less likely to be swayed by others' conjectural claims about what happened.

Here is an excerpt from a story about the harpooning that supports a claim at the stasis of definition (namely, that the whalers were inexperienced) with claims at the stasis of conjecture. Notice how closely connected claims of conjecture, definition, and value can be. And notice how different a sense of what happened this story gives from the Associated Press story presented earlier:

> The whalers' inexperience showed as the 30- to 40-ton carcass sank into the Pacific and was pulled by ocean currents more than three miles out to sea, dragging the motorboat along behind it.
>
> Divers raised the carcass back to the surface by lacing the whale's jaws shut and pumping compressed air into the body cavity. (*Daily Telegraph,* May 19, 1999)

The readers of the *Daily Telegraph* of London got a rather different answer to *What happened?* than did the readers of the AP story or the *New York Times.* Again, reasoning internally or externally at the stasis of conjecture suggests how far apart our experiences and perspectives can be.

This suggests how the stases can be used as a diagnostic tool: Studying the discourses of others and seeing that two parties have fundamental differences at the stasis of conjecture—or any stasis, for that matter—helps explain why no productive reasoning can go on at some points between particular individuals or groups. The debate in the United States over abortion is an example of one that has not moved forward because there is no agreement on fundamental conjectural and definitional issues, such as when life begins or whether women have a right to determine what happens to their bodies. Again, stasis theory offers a means of seeing different roads or paths of reasoning and where they may or may not lead.

How did this harpooning and the controversy surrounding it come to be? In other words, what caused it? The news stories give us various claims at the stasis of cause, as well, particularly because relatively few people knew about the issues behind the controversy.

What follows is a sampling of causal claims about the harpooning. Again, think of how these could all lead to paths of reasoning about the harpooning and its causes.

First, from the *Daily Telegraph* of London (May 19, 1999):

> Defying environmentalists who tried to stop their hunt, the Makah Indian tribe of Washington state have killed a gray whale for the first time in more than 70 years.
>
> The Makah, who have had to re-learn the art of whaling since they won permission to hunt last year, approached the whale in a hand-carved cedar canoe at dawn on Monday as the animal protectionists were asleep, and began the kill by throwing two eleven-foot harpoons.

Distilling this into its basic causal claims would yield something like this:

> The Makah were able to kill the whale because they relearned whaling and because the environmentalists were sleeping.

Again, these are causal claims and, like claims of conjecture or definition, are arguable. They could be otherwise.

A *Seattle Times* story (May 20, 1999) contained a different causal claim. Interviewed after he returned from killing the whale, Donny Swan, one of the Makah, said:

> There are no words to describe it. I felt the ancestors were out there spiritually. It happened at the right time and the right place. I think it was meant to be.

As the *Seattle Times* story made clear, however, claims of spirituality as a causal factor were behind the reasoning of the environmentalists as well as the Makah whalers:

> Paul Watson, the anti-whaling activist of the Sea Shepherd Conservation Society, whose 95-foot boat Sirenian threatened the hunt for months, took to fighting for whales after a bison appeared in a vision in 1973 and told him to protect "the bison of the sea."

In fact, the *Seattle Times* reporter made the topos of spirituality itself a causal factor in the news story:

> Spirituality was gasoline on the fire here, giving both sides a conviction without compromise. It transformed a few ragtag groups into organizations of incredible will and resolve.

Along with claims about cause, claims about possible consequences occur at the causal stasis. This suggests how causal arguments are similar to the common topos of *past fact, present fact, future fact.* Use this example from a *New York Times* story (May 18, 1999) about the harpooning to think about how claims of cause and consequence are similar to the common place of *past fact, present fact, future fact:*

> Representative Jack Metcalf, a Washington Republican and bitter critic of the hunt, said the killing could pave the way to an international assault on the whales.

Metcalf's causal claim depends on a sense of what has happened in the past, what is happening as he speaks, and what might happen in the future. This example also shows how claims of cause and consequence are similar to claims of conjecture, an issue we will return to in Chapter 3.

Thus far, we have looked at possible paths of reasoning at the stases of conjecture, definition, and cause. The disagreement between the Makah tribe and many environmentalists is, arguably, above all a disagreement at the stasis of value.

Here is one of several different value claims published in newspaper reports after the killing of the whale:

> In Vancouver, B.C., animal rights activist Peter Hamilton condemned the hunt as brutal and inhumane. "Anyone who enjoys subjecting an intelligent, sentient whale to an agonizing, slow death is a bloodthirsty savage," said Mr. Hamilton, founder of Lifeforce. (Ottawa *Citizen,* May 18, 1999)

This example makes two value claims, one about the hunt and one about the hunters.

This excerpt from *New York Times* coverage (May 18, 1999) of the story shows how the Makah and the environmentalists performed their values after the hunt was over:

> The emotional cultural clash sparked by the hunt was illustrated this evening by separate gatherings called to mark the event.
>
> The Makah were jubilant, and many of them described the event in mystical terms, citing a powerful reconnection with the whaling practice that had helped define their culture and that was the source of numerous legends, songs, traditions and tribal ceremonies. For centuries, it was a principal male rite of passage, and many Makah said the anticipation surrounding the hunt had been a huge inspiration for young people in the 1,700-member tribe.
>
> Protesters, who had come together in boats and on the shore at Neah Bay bearing signs that said "Tradition can be altered" and "Stop the killing," held mournful observances near the village and in downtown Seattle, nearly five hours away by car and ferry.

These different observances show how the killing of the whale was valued differently by the two parties. However, stasis theory again suggests that many kinds of claims can be made about issues of common concern—not merely *Are you for it or against it?*

The protesters' signs, while certainly not full-blown proposal arguments, do make claims at the stasis of procedure, as does the following excerpt, again from coverage in the *New York Times* (May 18, 1999):

> The Makah tribal leaders said they would kill whales only for subsistence and ceremonial purposes, and said that all the meat, blubber and oil from today's kill would be distributed among tribal members. Though they have the right, under the whaling commission's decision, to kill up to 20 whales for the next five years, they said they had no plans to try to sell whale meat or parts on the international market. They also do not currently have permission to do so.

This final example suggests the close connection between proposal arguments and the common topos of *past fact, present fact, future fact.*

Indeed, together, the topoi and stases enable you to build a map of reasoning. Historian of philosophy Richard McKeon wrote about this potential of rhetoric and called it "architectonic" (*Rhetoric: Essays in Invention and Discovery,* 1987). That is to say, in McKeon's view, rhetoric allows for the production of **archai,** or first principles upon which not only arguments but entire philosophies, systems, and worlds can be built. This is what rhetorician David Kaufer suggested by his claim that rhetoric is a design art (*Rhetoric and the Arts of Design,* 1996, with Brian Butler)—that is, an art that, as we discussed in terms of world-building in Chapter 1, allows entire systems to be invented and analyzed before they are literally built. Together, the stases and topoi allow reasoners like you to see the strengths, weaknesses, and possible consequences of paths and structures of human reasoning before they are carried out.

Rhetoric allows us as humans to invent potential worlds, reason about them, and then, perhaps, judge them unfit. Again, reasoning is a powerful—and too little utilized—process. Whether you imagine your inventional map as a road map or a topographic map or a flight map, reasoning allows you to use your inventions as inroads into terra incognita. In addition, reasoning allows you to imagine what awaits you down that road. Using reasoning and judgment, you may decide, "Let's not go there."

Structures of Reasoning

We have discussed the paths and places of reasoning. Let's now discuss some basic structures of reasoning. Again, by combining these ways of practicing reason, you can reason more clearly internally and more effectively externally. Like the stases and topoi, the following concepts provide ways of making sense of the sometimes deafening roar of discourse around us.

The basic strategy of reasoning is to start with an observation, or **claim**—an assertion or denial—and then offer some reason or evidence to **support** the observation or claim. It is true that people who offer good reasons or solid evidence for their assertions or denials do not always succeed in reasoning productively with or persuading others. But, ultimately, reasoned argument is more likely to be persuasive than discourse that relies on loud insistence, charm, or bullying. Besides, using the basic strategy of **claim plus support** for external reasoning is the behavior worthy of creatures endowed with the ability to reason among themselves.

Although this basic strategy of arguing is fairly universal, there have been, through the ages, a number of different structures for executing this basic strategy. These various structures all attempt to accomplish the same end: to win acceptance, internally or externally, for a particular thesis or claim or conclusion or judgment. But these structures go about achieving this end in different ways. *Ultimately, the most effective reasoning combines these various strategies.*

When thinking about structures of reasoning, it is good to distinguish between **general** questions (theses) and **particular** questions (hypotheses). A famous example of a general question is *Should one marry?* and—its particular counterpart—*Should Cato marry?* General questions are often understood as philosophical questions. From the time of Aristotle, however, rhetoric has been understood as concerned with particular questions: *Is a particular person guilty or innocent? Should the polis go to war with Sparta? Is Pericles to be praised or blamed?* Distinguishing general questions from particular questions is an important facet of sound reasoning, both internally and externally.

Induction and the Example

One common structure of reasoning is the form that logicians call **induction** and rhetoricians call the **example.** We will treat induction first and then examine how it works rhetorically through the example.

The Latin roots of the word *induction* offer clues about how the inductive structure of reasoning works: *in* = into + *ducere* = to lead. Literally, *induction* means "to lead into." After noting a series of similar phenomena, we may draw some conclusion or make some generalization about all phenomena of that kind. In other words, after observing a number of similar examples of something, we are led into a conclusion about most or all examples of that kind.

When Thomas Henry Huxley was trying to explain the process of induction to a group of workers in the nineteenth century, he used the example of hard green apples. Every time he picked up a hard green apple and bit into it, Huxley said, he found that it was sour. It does not take many experiences of this kind for someone to draw the conclusion that all hard green apples are sour. We do not have to taste all the hard green apples in the world to draw this conclusion; after we have tasted a reasonable number of them and found them to be sour, we could reasonably conclude that it is probable, even likely, that most hard green apples are going to be sour. We can make this conclusion, of course, until we learn otherwise—until we visit that far-off island where all the hard green apples are sweet as honey.

This structure of reasoning by induction—through the accrual of examples—seems natural and universal. This way of reasoning seems so natural that, most of the time, we are not even aware that we are reasoning inductively. You walk toward your bed, for instance, and think about sitting down on it. It has always held your weight before: One particular experience after another has suggested the bed will hold your weight. Will it this time? Induction would suggest it will.

Here is a graphic representation of the inductive reasoning process:

$$1, 2, 3, 4, 5, 6, 7 \ldots \text{ inductive leap} \longrightarrow \text{conclusion}$$

The numerals represent the number of examples of a phenomenon, and the inductive leap bridges the gap between the last example studied or experienced and the conclusion drawn. Usually, the shorter the leap, the sounder the conclusion. That is, the more examples scrutinized, the more reliable the general conclusion drawn.

An inductive leap, no matter how small, always involves a tiny bit of faith in the process of reasoning. A so-called perfect induction appears to involve no inductive leap. For instance, on the first day of a class, if the teacher were to ask each student, in turn, where he or she was born, the teacher could legitimately declare that the data gathered in that survey reveal that 67 percent of the students in that class were born in Ohio. Assuming that the students gave true answers and that the teacher's math was correct (see the faith required?), the conclusion or generalization made from the data would be sound. Perfect induction, however, is less like reasoning and more like computation or counting. Still, it is another way to understand what I mean by *induction*—the accrual of particular phenomena or particular examples that lead you to a general conclusion.

My colleague recently told me that when he and his brother were visiting a hotel near Big Bend National Park, a storm caused the power to go out on the morning of their departure. Then, he said, after he and his brother stopped the next night at another hotel, another storm caused the power to go out the morning they departed that hotel. "What an interesting potential example of induction!" I told him. "Does a storm hit and the power go off everywhere you two visit?" Of course, he said no, but such coincidences are reminders of the powers and perils of inductive reasoning.

To draw a general conclusion from just a few examples is to risk making a *hasty generalization*—something that is so easy to be led into that each of us has probably made hundreds of them in our lifetimes. We cannot say, in the abstract, how many examples of a phenomenon we must consider if we want to avoid making a hasty generalization. If we got violently ill the first three times that we ate corn dogs with barbecue sauce but did not get ill when we ate corn dogs without barbecue sauce, it would be reasonable to conclude that we should hold the sauce. But if three of our friends complained that their copies of a particular CD skipped, we may or may not be justified in pronouncing publicly that this particular CD was poorly manufactured. Among the tens of thousands or more of CDs produced, three is probably not a sufficient number of cases to validate our judgment. But it might bear further investigation.

Similarly, making hasty generalizations is particularly dangerous when it involves groups of people with whom we are not familiar. U.S. tourists in France, for instance, all too often make generalizations about French people on the basis of just a few encounters. I recently received an e-mail from a friend who had just returned from a trip to France. Of his experience with French people, he said, "I think I was worn out from trying to communicate/understand the French. Many times I thought they were just being snobs, but Peggy assured me it was only cultural differences." Avoiding hasty generalizations in dealing with people of other cultures can go a great way in learning to reason with and among people who are different from you.

Another risk of inductive reasoning involves drawing conclusions from an unrepresentative sampling of a particular phenomenon. If we were doing a survey in a particular city on how the citizens were inclined to vote a month before the election, our sampling of the voters could be unrepresentative in a number of ways: Our sampling could have been done predominantly or exclusively among the members of a particular ethnic group; among the members of a particular economic group; among the members of a particular religious group; among people with a certain level of education; among a particular age group; among a particular neighborhood; and so on. Not having surveyed a wide enough range of voters would undoubtedly skew any generalization we might want to make about our survey results.

In order to have a representative sampling of any phenomenon, statisticians have carefully worked out mathematical formulas for ensuring a randomly selected group. The chance of getting an unrepresentative sampling through such random selection is very slight. Although we cannot guarantee that the generalization we draw from our random sample will be valid—no reasoning is certain, remember—the random sampling does reduce the chance that our generalization will be unrepresentative.

Induction, then, involves following particular examples that lead to a generalization. Induction is the process through which one of the basic means of persuasion, the example, operates. Let's take a look now at the main vehicle of induction—the *example*.

While reasoning by induction involves accruing a series of particulars and then making an inductive leap to a general conclusion, reasoning by example works somewhat differently. Aristotle, the first to write about the example, understood examples as rhetorical inductions. That is to say, examples were means of arguing from one particular case to another particular case, the case at hand. As rhetorician Gerard Hauser has explained, examples provide parallel cases that suggest to the reasoner what conclusion to reach based on an example from the past ("The Example in Aristotle's *Rhetoric*," 1968). An inference is still required; this time, the inference takes the form of *This case is similar enough to that case that the example is persuasive*. Notice again how the topos of *past fact, present fact, future fact* has similarities with the structure of the example.

Examples rarely make for sound reasoning by themselves. Think about why: Whether an example serves as a parallel case is highly arguable and depends on many factors, most of which are out of control of the reasoner. Examples most often easily call forth counterexamples, as well. Examples are most effective, then, when they are combined with other structures of reasoning.

Remember the earlier example about my colleague and his brother and the power going out in their hotel rooms? What if the storms were not the cause of the power outages? What if the brother's use of several grooming appliances simultaneously caused the power outages? If my colleague and his brother were trying to figure out what to do the next morning to avoid a power outage in their hotel room, they might want to think about the examples of the previous two mornings. Or perhaps chance is the causal factor here, and examples and induction are not helpful.

Deduction and the Enthymeme

Another basic way in which the human mind reasons is by **deduction.** Just as the etymology of the word *induction* reveals the fundamental way in which inductive reasoning operates, so the etymology of *deduction* reveals the fundamental way in which deductive reasoning proceeds. An induction leads into a generalization; a deduction leads away from or out of a generalization into a conclusion about a particular.

Remember walking toward your bed and, based on many past experiences, feeling pretty secure that it would hold your weight? Perhaps all those particulars have accrued into a general rule: *This bed holds my weight.* So this time you walk toward your bed and think about sitting down on it. Will it hold your weight this time? Deduction—in the form of a general statement that says *This bed (always) holds my weight*—would suggest it will. The laws of physics are a help here, too. But as chaos theory and relativity have suggested, the laws of physics are not as immutable as some scientists would have us think. (Still, I hope there's no chaos theory at play when you sit down on your bed!)

In our earlier discussion of Huxley's example of the hard green apples, we saw the way in which induction and deduction proceed. If every time we bite into a hard green apple we find the taste is sour, we very soon will be led into making the generalization that all hard green apples are sour, a taste that we do not relish. (If we made this statement in a group of people with different tastes, someone would be sure to say, "If you think all hard green apples are sour, you haven't tasted a Granny Smith apple!" Huxley didn't have those . . .) So the next time someone offers us a hard green apple, we may very well refuse it. Our reasoning, in this instance, follows this basic structure of premises leading to a conclusion:

> All hard green apples are sour.
>
> This apple is hard and green.
>
> Therefore, this apple must be sour.

This pattern of argument is traditionally known as a **syllogism.** As he was for so many other elements of reasoning, Aristotle was the first to formulate the structure of the syllogism. Medieval philosophers and teachers reduced and systematized the Aristotelian formulation of the syllogism. For centuries in the Western world, students were required to learn how to construct valid syllogisms and to detect the logical flaws in the syllogistic reasoning of others. The syllogism is a schematization of the structure by which the human mind reasons deductively, but it has very little to do with how people reason and argue in real life.

Although it is clear that people argue deductively every day of their lives, you will rarely, if ever, engage in or witness reasoning in which the participants exchange a series of syllogisms. Even Aristotle conceded that the syllogism is an artificial construction, useful in its own way but a rather unnatural method of conducting an argument in real life. Have you ever witnessed or participated in an argument in which one or more of the participants consistently enunciated two premises and a conclusion, the form of a syllogism? Probably not. But you likely have witnessed or participated in many arguments in which you or others have used another form resembling the syllogism—the **enthymeme.**

The enthymeme is of much more use than the syllogism in understanding and conducting reasoning and argument among other humans in day-to-day life. Again from the Greek, *enthymeme* means literally "in the thymus"—which requires a bit more explanation. The ancient Greeks thought the soul—which was not understood at the time as separate from the mind (recall our discussion of ethos, pathos, and logos in Chapter 1)—was located in the thymus gland in the neck. To reason enthymematically, then, was to reason in the mind or in the soul. As George Kennedy notes, Isocrates and Alcidamas used *enthymeme* to mean "ideas expressed in speech" (*Classical Rhetoric,* 1999).

What this means in terms of the structures of reasoning is that enthymemes have what we will call, for the moment, missing, or unstated, premises that are filled in by what the listeners or readers already think and feel. Enthymemes are thus the most realistic and helpful structure for understanding and constructing arguments with other people.

In his *Rhetoric,* Aristotle called the enthymeme a "rhetorical syllogism." This notion of what is often called a *truncated* syllogism accords with Aristotle's notion that the enthymeme represents how the vast majority of people reason deductively. Ordinary people do not have the patience or concentration to follow all the steps of a full deductive argument, formally valid syllogism after formally valid syllogism after formally valid syllogism. For this reason, most deductive reasoning happens instead through enthymemes.

Here is an example of an argument in the form of an enthymeme:

Josh is a happy person because he is smiling all the time.

Here, the person uttering the statement is inferring something about the disposition of Josh from the observation that he smiles all the time. The clause *Josh is a happy person* states the conclusion of the process of reasoning that the person came to. The dependent clause *because he's smiling all the time* gives one of this person's reasons for coming to this conclusion. Another reason for this conclusion, however, is implied, rather than explicitly stated. It can be deduced from what is explicitly stated. Can you figure it out?

The reason that is implied, rather than explicitly stated, is *Anyone who smiles all the time is a happy person.* If we were to reconstruct a formal syllogism from this enthymeme, the syllogism would look something like this:

Anyone who smiles all the time must be happy.

Josh is a person who smiles all the time.

Therefore, Josh is a happy person.

Although this syllogism is formally valid—it has all the right parts in the right order—many people would still not agree with it. They may very well—and very reasonably—reject the conclusion because they doubt the truth of one of the premises. If they knew Josh, they might agree that he smiles all the time, but they might reject as false the general proposition that *Anyone who smiles all the time is a happy person.*

People invent and utter enthymemes all the time without being aware that they are reasoning deductively. This, then, is the basic structure of an enthymeme:

Conclusion

Because

Reason

Although basically every enthymeme includes a conclusion and a statement supporting that conclusion, enthymemes can take several forms. All of the following are enthymemes, but note the variety of forms in which they are expressed. In some of them, the nature and relationship of the claims are indicated explicitly, while in others we have to figure out which proposition states the conclusion and which states one of the supporting reasons. Note the differences:

1. Don't tell me that he's a great running back, **for** he gained over 100 yards only twice this season.
2. **Since** he goes kayaking, he must be a nature boy.
3. Those Michigan students probably were in Fort Lauderdale **because** they're so tanned this early in the spring.
4. That must be the most popular movie of the year. It grossed $85 million in the first two weeks after its release.
5. The most convincing argument that cigarette smoking is bad for your health is that a large percentage of smokers die from lung cancer.
6. He drives a Mercedes-Benz, **so** he must be rich.
7. David failed three courses this semester; **thus,** he must not have studied very hard.
8. Murph is definitely running a temperature. Look how flushed her face is!
9. If he's got schnauzers, he must be a nice guy.

Words such as *for, since,* and *because* signal that the sentence that follows states a reason or grounds for the conclusion that came first. Words like *so, thus,* and *therefore* signal that the sentence that follows articulates a conclusion or claim. In the absence of such signaling words, we as readers or listeners must be able to figure out which part of the statement constitutes the conclusion and which constitutes support for the conclusion.

In an enthymeme such as *Murph is definitely running a temperature. Look how flushed her face is,* we must be practiced enough reasoners to be able to figure out that the clause *Murph is definitely running a temperature* is the conclusion and that the flushed face is the evidence or premise from which the conclusion is drawn. The same would be true of any other enthymeme lacking explicit signaling words that designate how the clauses of the enthymeme are related.

Once we are able to determine what the conclusion is and what the supporting premise is, we can test the enthymeme for its rhetorical soundness. Many times, we find that it is the unstated premise behind our reasoning that makes our enthymeme unsound. For instance, in our Mercedes-Benz example, the assumption that anyone who drives such an expensive automobile is rich may be the questionable part of the reasoning. Or maybe we cannot decide whether we agree or disagree with the assumption until we get a definition of what *rich* means in this context—particularly to the person we are reasoning with! For inventing our own reasoning and for detecting shortcomings in the reasoning of others, understanding enthymemes is crucial.

Missing Premises and From Whom They Are Missing

Understanding enthymemes helps you structure your own reasoning and helps you follow and analyze the reasoning of others. Again, remember the structure of an enthymeme:

Conclusion

Because

Reason

Very often, as in the Mercedes-Benz example, another premise is required to make the conclusion sound, but very often that other premise will be unstated. Here is an example I use very often in class to explain the idea of the missing premise of an enthymeme and its intimate connection to audience:

> Magda is a good roommate
>
> because
>
> Magda is tolerant.

In this formal presentation of an enthymeme, the missing, or unstated, premise is what? *Anyone who is tolerant is a good roommate.* Might I suggest that such a premise is not something that all audiences would assent to? For instance, if you are telling your friends about your roommate being tolerant, they may agree with your general rule about anyone who is tolerant being a good roommate. But your parents may disagree with the general premise—or they may want more information about what you mean by *tolerant:* Tolerant of what? Religious differences? Strong odors? A collection of geese? The point is, the enthymeme does not have a missing premise unless the audience fails to provide it! Your hearer or reader is thus an essential part of your reasoning process when you reason enthymematically.

This understanding of the enthymeme as always resonating with the hearer or reader is informed as well by conceptions of rhetoric from the twentieth century. Kenneth Burke's idea that identification should replace persuasion as a way of understanding human reason (*A Rhetoric of Motives*, 1950) suggests that before we can change someone else's mind—or before we can change our own minds—we need to have some way of identifying with the agent of change. All division and no identification leads to stagnation. Perelman and Olbrechts-Tyteca, too, understood the role of the listener or reader in reasoning when they said that all argument begins in agreement (*The New Rhetoric*, 1969).

Aristotle also had an understanding of how this works. In his treatise *On the Soul*, he distinguished *potential* from *actualized* states. A central question of his treatise concerns what animates something or moves it from its potential state to an actualized state. One way to understand the structure of the enthymeme is that it actualizes some potential in hearers or readers. This view of reasoning as actualizing helps explain, as we discussed in Chapter 1, how ethos, pathos, and logos work together.

Again, the power of the enthymeme for invention is that it structurally incorporates the listener or reader into the process of reasoning. The missing premise of the enthymeme, then, can be the means through which two parties find common ground—or recognize that they have none. That, perhaps, is a place to start talking.

Toulmin: The Enthymeme Unfurled

Stephen Toulmin, a twentieth-century British philosopher, proposed an alternative to both the system of deductive reasoning that Aristotle had invented and the system of deduction that mathematical logicians had proposed in the first decades of the twentieth century. Instead of basing his system of practical reasoning on mathematics, Toulmin's book *The Uses of Argument* (1958) is based on the kind of arguments that are used in legal reasoning—the same source that gave us, millennia earlier, the stases. Fundamentally, the Toulmin system would be concerned with the strength of the case that we present in support of our claims. It is the metaphor of **case** that betrays the affinity of Toulmin's system of reasoning with the kind of arguments that lawyers present in the courtroom. What Toulmin's system does, in essence, is open the enthymeme and its various premises even further, allowing reasoners to study and invent and plan arguments in great detail before they begin to argue.

Here is a dialogue that could take place between two friends about a mutual acquaintance:

> "I'll just bet you that Michael O'Malley is Catholic."
>
> "Why do you say that?"
>
> "Well, I know he is an Irishman born in Southern Ireland."
>
> "So what?"
>
> "People born in Southern Ireland are almost certain to be Catholic."
>
> "What's your support for that statement?"
>
> "Well, I read in the London Times the other day that 93 percent of Irish people born in the southern part of Ireland are Roman Catholics."
>
> "Couldn't Mike be one of the 7 percent who aren't Catholic?"

"Yes, I suppose he could. And even if he was born Catholic, he might not still follow the faith now. That's why I said that the Irish born in the South of Ireland are *almost* certain to be Catholic!"

Before we examine the reasoning going on in this dialogue, we need to know some of Toulmin's terminology—just as we needed to familiarize ourselves with the terms Aristotle and others used for the stases, the topoi, the example, and the enthymeme.

The term that Toulmin uses to designate the conclusion of a process of reasoning is **claim**. A **datum** is a fact or conjecture or reason that prompts someone to make a claim. A **warrant** supports or authenticates the datum. Further support for the supporting warrant Toulmin calls **backing**. A **qualifier** is some word or phrase that indicates the force or the extent of the claim. An exception is called a **rebuttal.**

Here is a graphic representation of the Toulmin system of reasoning. It might help you to think of it as an enthymeme on its side, where the claim is the conclusion and the datum and other components are elements of the reasons:

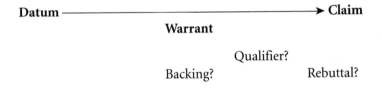

Now we can apply the Toulmin terms to the various propositions advanced in the dialogue just presented. The *claim* the first speaker makes is that Michael O'Malley is probably Catholic. In response to the other speaker's question, the first speaker cites a *datum,* or perceived fact, that has prompted him to make his claim. The *warrant* is what gives supporting significance to the fact cited about O'Malley's birthplace:

Virtually all people born in the southern part of Ireland are Roman Catholic.

This warrant is, in turn, authenticated by the *backing,* a report in a responsible newspaper of some kind of a survey that indicated the extraordinarily high percentage of Southern Irish who are Catholic. But there is a *qualifier* and a potential exception, or *rebuttal,* to the first speaker's claim. The qualifier appears in the phrase that limits the extent of the claim: *almost certain.* The rebuttal that would invalidate the first speaker's claim is the possibility that their acquaintance may be either a lapsed Catholic or part of that small percentage of Irish born in the south who are not Roman Catholic.

Many people find the Toulmin scheme of argument much easier to understand and use than Aristotle's syllogism. And the statements of the argument strike most people as being expressed in more natural language than the often artificial language of the premises and conclusion of a reconstructed Aristotelian syllogism. What is missing in the Toulmin system is a set of rules or guidelines for assessing the quality of the argument. Toulmin seems to suggest that common sense will reveal where an argument has gone awry. After all, jurors, who are usually not trained in the fine points of the law, are often able to assess the soundness of the arguments presented in the courtroom by lawyers for the prosecution and defense.

Thus, many people feel more comfortable with Toulmin's method of plotting an argument than with Aristotle's method. But the Toulmin system is not as straightforward as it may appear. Confronted with the text of an argument, readers or listeners must still be able to discriminate in the sequence of sentences the claim from the datum and the warrant from the backing if they want to analyze and judge the reasoning.

What is particularly important to emphasize about Toulmin's system is that court cases are decided not based on proven fact but on probabilities. As we discussed earlier, rhetoric, as an art, grew out of the need for people in ancient Greece to reason effectively in language with each other about that which could be otherwise—in the context of Toulmin's system, whether a citizen charged with an offense was guilty or not. Even today—especially given a legal system in which the defendant is presumed innocent until proven guilty and in which he or she cannot be forced to give testimony that may be detrimental to his or her case—most cases are decided on the basis of probabilities. Often in murder trials, for instance, only the accused—and perhaps a supreme being—knows for sure whether he or she committed the crime. The prosecutor must argue the case in such a way that it will appear highly probable to the jury that the accused did indeed perpetrate the murder, and the defense must argue the case in such a way that it will appear highly probable that the accused did not, could not, or would not commit the crime.

From Invention to Judgment

This chapter of inventional tools—places, paths, and structures of reasoning—can generate quite a load of reasoning. Recall that the end (as in the goal or destination) of reasoning is judgment—however ephemeral. Thus, along with practicing invention, we need to practice making judgments—both individual and collective.

Stases and Time

Building on our discussion of kronos and kairos, let's now look at stasis theory more generally, focusing on the issue of time. Stasis theory came first from courtroom rhetoric, which involved **forensic** questions, or questions about what had happened in the **past.** Like forensic medicine, which inquires into how a dead body came to be dead, forensic rhetoric asks questions about what happened in the past and what is just or unjust, given what happened in the past.

Conjectural claims, however, like stasis theory in general, can work in situations other than just forensic ones. Conjectures can address **epideictic** questions, or questions about the **present;** epideictic questions address what values a community shares at the present time. Examples of epideictic rhetoric include everything from popular songs to obituaries. Conjectures can also address **deliberative** questions, or questions about the **future.**

Stasis questions started in forensic rhetoric—What happened in the past? But all the stases can function for deliberative and epideictic questions, as well—What should we do? and What are our shared values now? What arguments are likely to move which audiences? Which arguments are ethical and which pander to the audience, just making them believe what flatters them? What kind of reasoning does not exploit power imbalances but includes all parties equitably? These concepts can help you come up with a great deal to think about and, potentially, to write and to say. But along with knowing what arguments you can get out, practice knowing which ones you should put away.

❖ *Reasoning Practice*

Before we move on to Chapter 3, which discusses claims of conjecture in detail, you need to practice recognizing and internalizing the stases and topoi, using induction and deduction, and applying the other central rhetorical concepts we discussed in this chapter.

1. Use the concepts in this chapter to invent things to say about the following statement from the Ottawa *Citizen* (May 18, 1999):

    In Vancouver, B.C., animal rights activist Peter Hamilton condemned the hunt as brutal and inhumane. "Anyone who enjoys subjecting an intelligent, sentient whale to an agonizing, slow death is a bloodthirsty savage," said Mr. Hamilton.

2. Review the discourses about the whale controversy in this chapter and consider these questions:
    - What common topoi were used?
    - What specific topoi emerged about the whale controversy as a particular subject of discourse?

3. Find a piece of public discourse—a newspaper report full of direct quotations, a transcript of a news show on radio or television, or an editorial or op-ed column (letters to the editor will likely be too short for this assignment)—and consider the following questions:
    - Find a claim at each of the stases.
    - Make a list of the topoi raised in the report or editorial.
    - Find an example in the discourse. Is it used to argue from particular to particular or from particular to general?
    - Find a few enthymemes. List the conclusions and the supporting premises. What are the missing, or unstated, premises? When there are no unstated premises, reason about why. Note how the Toulmin system of reasoning enables you to describe parts of the article. Given the enthymemes, the warrants, the backing, what guesses can you make about who might be the listeners or hearers of the discourse?

4. Read the following wire service report from the *Austin American-Statesman* (January 2000), and see how many places, paths, and structures of reasoning you can find in it. Then write or prepare to talk about how any part of the short article might work toward or against identification.

Fortune magazine recently used the career arcs of Mort Topfer and George Fisher to draw a quick sketch of what's happened in U.S. business in recent years. The two spent 18 years together at Motorola until the mid-'90s, when "Fisher left to take the helm of Kodak, a true-blue blue chip. Topfer left to join upstart Dell." While Fisher has made about $74 million at Kodak, Topfer has earned about $694 million, mostly in Dell stock options. Fisher says he has no regrets: "I think we all make more than we know what to do with."

3

Conjectures

Places to Begin

The Primary Stasis

What does the noun *conjecture* suggest to you? A guess? An account? A story? Anything at all?

Conjecture came to modern English from Latin through Old French and Middle English. In contemporary usage, it describes an inference made from incomplete information. The Latin, meanwhile, suggests that a conjecture is an interpretation, a mental putting-together of things in a way that could be otherwise. While the conjectural stasis provides a place to begin the process of reasoning, only relatively rarely does a conjectural claim become the central claim of an entire argument. This chapter, in addition to introducing you to some forms conjectural claims can take, will acquaint you with some of the wide-ranging functions of claims at the stasis of conjecture.

For practitioners and theorists of the stasis questions, conjecture usually comes first. Its primary position suggests that shared assumptions about the facts of any case—whether empirically verified or not—are necessary for productive reasoning at other stases to proceed. We can also understand these shared assumptions as manifesting identification; as you might remember from Chapter 1, some kind of identification is

49

necessary for any collaborative external reasoning to proceed. In that way, conjectural claims themselves are inventional because they can help reasoners find a beginning point from which to generate possible common claims at conjecture as well as at other stases. *This happened to me* may become *This happened to us; This happened to us* may become *We will see that this never happens again.*

Though they are primary, conjectural claims rarely receive the attention they merit in textbooks on reasoning and argument because conjectural claims transcend foundational distinctions in Western thought. Textbooks often divide rhetoric from poetry as well as from dialectic or philosophy, but this book endeavors to bring those traditions together again for the purpose of helping people learn both to study and to engage in practical reasoning. My goal in this chapter is to enable you to recognize how elemental to reasoning conjectural claims are. So in this chapter, we will look at conjectural claims as they function in practical reasoning of various sorts.

Conjectural claims set out to answer at least one of two related questions:

What happened?

Does a particular shared reality exist?

As we discussed in Chapter 2, reasoning at the stasis of conjecture suggests that humans do not always agree on what constitutes a fact. Because we are limited by space and time—by our bodies and their locations and by what we can perceive at a given time in space—we have no Archimedean point from which to grasp the "real" facts or to see what "really" happened. Human beings' situatedness makes absolute knowledge impossible for us to maintain in time: We are embodied reasoners, deliberating bodies. Whether embodiedness is truly a limit is beyond our scope in this book.

Conjectures are among the most contentious and fraught kinds of claims externally. Internally, conjecture claims are often more straightforward: If you saw something with your eyes or heard it with your ears or felt it with your own skin, you are less likely to be swayed by others' conjectural claims about what happened. On the other hand, being somewhere and experiencing events firsthand might have its limitations, as well: Being a participant in an event limits your ability to perceive the whole—or even to perceive situations other than your own. As one of William Faulkner's characters reasoned, "If I had been there, I couldn't have seen it this plain."

A Trove of Conjectural Claims

Before we discuss conjectural claims further, let's look at a trove of them. These conjectural claims are from the "Old Town Police Log," as published in the July 15, 1999, *Penobscot Times* in Old Town, Maine—a community that, I would guess, likes to share its conjectures. (These items are listed here just as they were in the *Penobscot Times*, with individual police cases separated by ellipses.)

> **Monday, June 28**—At 3:37 a.m. police arrested a juvenile for a theft on S. Main St.; the report contained no other information, except to say charges were pending . . . A Milford woman wanted another woman to stop calling her; the two ladies had been having trouble getting along for a while; an officer tried to call the apparent caller, but her phone had been disconnected . . . Police handled four minor complaints about animals . . . A Lincoln St. man called police after witnessing kids rip the screen off a door at Meadow Lane; police spoke to the owner of the residence in question, who said that some kids had come over and were arguing, and damaged her door out of frustration; she said she did not want to press charges because her daughter was partly to blame . . . A Poplar St. woman complained that a man had called her asking for money her husband owes him; she said she told him she wanted nothing to do with the situation because it's between the two of them; the man then asked her if she was aware that her husband "is trying to sleep with my wife," and then hung up; police contacted the man and told him to contact his lawyer or go to small claims court if he has a problem collecting bills; the sheriff's department had already warned him for similar behavior . . . A Spring St. woman said [she] heard two gunshots; police found nothing suspicious in the area, and said the noise could have been thunder . . . Police responded to two false alarms . . . Juveniles were reported riding bicycles in and out of traffic on Center St. at 11:44 p.m., but were gone when police responded.

Tuesday, June 29—A speeding vehicle reported on French Island at 1:23 a.m. was never located; one officer searching for the vehicle saw a similar one and stopped it on Center St.; the operator denied speeding on French Island; a [Department of Motor Vehicles] check revealed that her license was under suspension, and the officer issued a summons for this violation . . . A resident saw a suspicious vehicle at the high school at 1:41 in the morning; an officer found two people playing basketball, and informed them that school property closes at 11 p.m.; they left promptly . . . A N. Main St. man said he was having a problem with his ex-wife, who lives in Hampden; she had been spreading information that said he was a bad businessman; she was even distributing flyers; police asked him to keep them posted if anything else happened . . . A Bodwell St. man found a black purse at the base of a lilac bush in his yard; he soon discovered that it belonged to his neighbor's daughter, who perhaps left it on top of her car by accident . . . A Front St. man complained that a rottweiler attacked his dog on River St.; he said he was walking his dog on a leash, looking for a cat in people's back yards, when the rottweiler broke its chain and came after his dog; witnesses told a different story, though; they said he was walking through people's back yards with a child and his dog, which was not on a leash, and his dog charged the rottweiler, which was minding its own business, and bit it, then ran away; anxious to retaliate, the rottweiler then broke its chain and went after the complainant's dog, neighbors said; a bystander separated the two animals; their owners said the dogs' shots were up-to-date; police warned the complainant for letting a dog run at large and for walking in other people's yards without their permission . . . A Bradley man reported a mother duck with ducklings attempting to cross S. Main St.; but the family was gone before an officer could get there. . . .

In the words of humorist Dave Barry, "I AM NOT MAKING THIS UP!!!"

The portion of the police log you just read took up fewer than 10 column inches of newspaper type; the issue of the *Penobscot Times* from which I took this excerpt featured roughly 50 column inches of police log. So what you read above constitutes less than one-fifth of the conjectural claims about what happened in Old Town during just one week.

Most of the claims in the police log function as straightforward claims about what happened. A few of them, however, also make claims about whether a shared reality can be said to exist. Let's look at a few in detail.

> At 3:37 a.m. police arrested a juvenile for a theft on S. Main St.;
> the report contained no other information, except to say charges
> were pending.

This item from the police log answers both what happened—"police arrested a juvenile"—and whether a shared reality exists: "Charges were pending" posits the reality of a law enforcement system whose consequences are shared by community members. This item also suggests how conjectures can be about the past, the present, or the future, a point we will return to at the end of this chapter.

> A Milford woman wanted another woman to stop calling her;
> the two ladies had been having trouble getting along for a while;
> an officer tried to call the apparent caller, but her phone had been
> disconnected.

Did you notice that the second conjectural claim in this series, which makes a generalization that provides background information, contains the word *ladies* rather than *girls* or *women*? What does that word choice suggest? Did the police log writer just use a different word to avoid repeating the same noun three times? (*Women, women, women?*) Is that any excuse? We need a conjectural claim to say what might have happened. And how did the phone get disconnected? Since there is no reason listed, citizens of Old Town are left, well, to conjecture: Were there other people the caller called too often? Did those other people somehow have her phone disconnected? Was it a plot? This series of conjectural claims suggests how quickly conjectures can foster narratives.

Conjectural claims, through their very partiality, leave openings for additional questions as well as other claims at the conjectural stasis and at other stases. They can fall into the kind of pattern suggested by the journalist's mantra: *Who? What? Where?* and *When?* The final question in that litany—*How?*—suggests that cause and conjecture are related, a point we will save for Chapter 5.

Police handled four minor complaints about animals.

This conjectural claim is the result of observation; it provides a generalization based on counting and classifying. Conjectural claims often give rise to more conjectural claims in the form of generalizations. After reading the police log, a citizen might observe to a neighbor, "We have some kind of animal problem here in Old Town." Again, conjectures can establish a sense of shared reality. But what does it mean to *handle?* We will have to guess.

Indeed, after some internal reasoning of your own, you might recognize the close affiliation between claims of conjecture and claims of definition. Conjectures and definitions share substantial ground: If we have words to describe something, at least in some senses that thing can be said to exist—particularly if we think of words as a means of establishing a shared reality. Yet which words we choose to describe something can make a huge difference in how we—and others—perceive the thing.

Claims about what something looks like or sounds like in an effort to answer *What happened?* also suggest just how closely related conjectural and definitional claims are when they describe or categorize. "It sounded like a freight train" is a frequent answer to reporters' questions after a tornado. These kinds of claims also suggest how metaphors and similes are related to claims of conjecture. "My love is like a red, red rose." Well . . . yes and no. Indeed, conjectural claims reveal the arbitrary nature not only of names but of all language—points we will return to in Chapter 4, when we study definitional claims.

Consider this claim from the "Old Town Police Log":

A Spring St. woman said [she] heard two gunshots; police found nothing suspicious in the area, and said the noise could have been thunder.

Perhaps this woman—not, apparently, a *lady*—said, "Well, officer, it sounded kind of like thunder." Or perhaps not. For us at least, it's a matter of conjecture—for now, anyway.

How to Spot a Conjectural Claim

Unlike claims of definition and evaluation, which have linking verbs connecting their subjects with their predicates, conjectural claims have active verbs when they answer the question *What happened?* Let's look at a few more from the *Penobscot Times*:

> A canoeist flipped over near the Gilman Falls Dam; an officer arrived to find a man loading a canoe on his truck; he said he had flipped over and was "giving up" for the day.

Hear the verbs? *Flipped over, arrived, said, giving up.* Again, when conjectures claim that something has happened, is happening, or will happen, they usually require active, rather than linking, verbs.

One more police log goodie, for now:

> A N. Main St. man said he was having a problem with his ex-wife, who lives in Hampden; she had been spreading information that said he was a bad businessman; she was even distributing flyers; police asked him to keep them posted if anything else happened.

I wonder whether this is the woman who heard gun shots. Or maybe it is the lady who was being harassed by phone calls. Hard to know. Any conjectures about why this is the only item in which the police want the complainant to "keep them posted"?

I can't resist; here's one more:

> Anxious to retaliate, the rottweiler then broke its chain and went after the complainant's dog, neighbors said.

Any conjectures about how the police reporter—or the neighbors—knew the dog was "anxious to retaliate"?

The vast majority of conjectures may very well have nothing to support them. Often, they are uttered without explicit intention:

> That turtle managed to cross the highway.

Still, conjectures function as potential support for many other claims. This dual role makes them very much worth studying and using.

Conjectures are as ubiquitous as air.

Three Types of Conjectural Claims

Precisely because they are so common, conjectural claims take many forms. We will concentrate here on three: **observations, expressions,** and **narratives.** Conjectural claims function as starts for invention, as means of setting off down a possible road or of clearing a possible path. In addition, conjectural claims support other claims when a reasoner is further down a path and is looking for motivation to stay a particular course.

One final preliminary word: Conjectural claims tend to change their classification depending on what function they are understood to serve. A narrative can end up as an example when it is used to support another claim; eloquent expression can be repeated in a way that might make it literature; forensic conjectures, if they endure in public memory, become history. Conjectures are as consequential as they are common.

Observations

Conjectural claims often take the form of *observations*—for instance:

> There was a fly in my soup.
>
> You look like you're going to fall off that chair.
>
> He was a white man in a pink shirt.
>
> I am tired of this system of things.

Here's a weird one:

> Once my parents and I had lunch at a relatively bohemian inn located in rural Pennsylvania. Though I maintain that my father did not tell me so that day, he claimed later that there had been dog dirt on the floor of the restaurant while we were eating there.

Let me be clear: I do remember flies. Plenty of 'em. Because of the flies alone, I knew lunch was ruined for my dad, but I observed no dog dirt and heard no discourses about dog dirt. For me, that dog dirt has never existed. That is as far as shared reasoning can go.

Precisely because even statements that are not intended to be arguable have potential consequences for others, conjectural statements often prompt arguments. (No, I never reasoned with my father about whether the substance in question had actually been on the floor of the restaurant. What's the point of a "Was so," "Was not," "Was so," "Was not" kind of conversation? A cruise to nowhere.) Figuring out the possible productive directions for reasoning when faced with a clash of conjectural claims is one of the powers you can develop by practicing reasoning using the stasis questions. For better or worse, I have just turned one clash of conjectural claims into a narrative.

Imagine two people in a building. One of them says, "It's hailing." The other one says, "No it's not; I can't hear it." They both go and see whether it is hailing. As this hypothetical example suggests, a conjecture is a fact when two or more individuals agree on the conjecture in question. A conjecture is a fact to the extent that it has been verified.

The chaotic public conversation about whether global warming is happening provides a real-life example of how fundamental rhetorical reasoning at the stasis of conjecture is. While some experts say global warming is verifiable fact, others say that global warming is not happening—no way, no how. Until parties can agree on a procedure for finding shared conjectures, no fact can be said to exist, no matter how empirically true particular pieces of evidence seem to be. And until there is a process for finding shared conjectures, there is little hope for any coherent public policy about global warming.

Illustrations of the inventional power of the stasis questions often begin with this ancient forensic example, one that underscores the primacy of conjectural claims:

> A person charges another person in court with stealing his urn. The defendant says he did not steal the urn, arguing at the stasis of conjecture. This yields no productive ground. What options for productive argument do the stasis questions suggest?

Arguing at the stasis of definition, the defendant might claim that he did not steal the urn; rather, he might argue, he borrowed it—supporting his reasoning with further support for his claim. (The defendant might also argue that the item in question was not an urn, but outside rhetoric class, this would probably not result in an acquittal!)

Or the defendant might say he did steal the urn but he did so for morally good purposes; his daughter was dying and needed a particularly costly medicine and he had no money. This argument would either have to depend on enthymemes of value that the judges already share or the defendant would have to argue and support his value claim that moral law is higher than civil law.

Finally, the judges might throw the urn case out because it has been brought before the wrong court or because it has no merit. Or the judges might find the defendant guilty and order him into exile. Or the judges might find the defendant innocent and suggest the parties go celebrate—or mourn, as the case may be. These moves are at the stasis of procedure.

In any case, all those various claims about the urn were set in motion by one conjectural observation: *He stole my urn.*

Expressions

I'm thirsty. I feel dehydrated.

I love you.

You make me tired.

I feel like dancing.

Your world frightens and confuses me.

A wild heart cannot be broken.

These are *expressions,* claims of affect about a self to another. Many conjectural claims are not meant to be arguable because they rely solely on individual experiences and preferences and are not necessarily the result of intention. And experiences that are intense or fraught or painful often are least likely to find expression at all.

Expressions can serve a very important role in internal reasoning. Listening to your own expressions enables you to spot recurring topoi in your life and to examine what paths and roads you frequent—as well as to imagine what might be your terra incognita, places of reasoning where you consistently do not go, paths that you have never taken. Diary writing, free association, brainstorming, and other invention exercises—along with conversation—can help reasoning through expressions to begin. Sometimes, merely expressing oneself in writing or speech provides a means to begin reasoning; other times, when reasoning has stalled, expressions are a way to jump-start it again.

Yet the transition from private or personal expression to external reasoning is a complicated one. Telling yourself "I feel very warm" or "I really enjoyed that ballgame" can be very different from telling someone else the same thing. In everyday life, humans regularly deliberate internally what expressions they should or should not verbalize or write to others. Uttered or written expressions can also halt reasoning, particularly when external reasoning is under way:

What you wrote in your last e-mail really bothers me.

Reasoning can take many paths and directions from there, some of which likely would not be productive.

Putting experience into language is a complex process, and I cannot hope to address the nature or scope of that process here. My point is rather that expressions are kinds of discourse that, while conjectural, profoundly affect reasoning of all kinds. Identifying expressions and coming to understand and use them are parts of practicing the elements of reasoning. We are social beings, and it behooves us to understand our various shared means of reasoning and attempt to use them all to our best purposes.

Expressions of pain, in particular, usually do not make their way easily into external reasoning. Some scholars of public discourse have even argued that pain is not an appropriate thing to talk about in public because there is no easy response to affect. Yet just because no easy response suggests itself does not mean expressions of pain, individual or collective, should not be welcomed into processes of reasoning. Expressing experiences in shared language (external reasoning) or in language that could be shared (internal reasoning) provides a place from which reasoning among people of diverse backgrounds and generations might proceed.

Some expressions are so eloquent that they become literature. The poem that serves as the epigraph for this book is an example of an expression that has long been defined as literature. The poem's other conjectures—observations that accrue into an anecdote—culminate in the speaker's elliptical expression, "For once, then, something." Popular songs often become eloquent expressions of particular times or particular groups, and some expressions of fictional characters capture the imagination of many people, becoming shorthand for our own conjectures. From J. J. Walker's "dy-no-mite" in the 1970s to Homer Simpson's "d'oh" in the 1990s, others' expressions have a way of finding their way into our minds and mouths:

> Go ahead: make my day.
>
> Show me the money.

Here's one from World War II:

> Oversexed, overpaid, and over here.

I said earlier that experiences that are profound, fraught, or painful are often unlikely to find expression. Yet expressions also are sometimes so eloquent—they speak so well the unexpressed for a group at a point in time—that they retain a place in public memory. Neil Armstrong's expression when he landed on the moon, an expression he maintains was the result of no forethought whatsoever, has certainly found a place in the memories of generations:

> That's one small step for man, and one giant leap for mankind.

That inventional expressions serve an important function in shared reasoning is not a new idea. Indeed, in the early sixteenth century, the writer Erasmus composed a handbook of expressions, *De Copia,* or *About Abundance,* to help people learn how to have a ready supply of utterances when they needed to have something to say—or write. One section of *De Copia,* for instance, offers over 100 ways to say or write "Your letter pleased me mightily" to a friend.

Though I am no Erasmus, I was thinking of my friend Anne the other day and roughly these thoughts escaped me: I never apologized to her for the many nights, now nearly 20 years ago, when I said I would stay up all night studying with her for our Shakespeare class. I always fell asleep after a few minutes of trying to read, and she would study on—by herself—for hours. So I said out loud, as though apologizing to her: "For all the nights I slept and you read Shakespeare, I am sorry."

And then I began to think of not *different* ways of saying the same thing like Erasmus did but of how uttering the same expression in a slightly different way can be understood—conjecturally—very differently. Consider:

> For all the nights I slept and you read Shakespeare, I am sorry.
>
> For all the nights you read Shakespeare while I slept, I am sorry.
>
> All the nights you read Shakespeare and I slept; I am sorry.
>
> All the nights I slept for you read Shakespeare.

As I said, I'm no Erasmus. But I appreciate the point that conjectural expressions, even without intention, can leave different readers and listeners with very different understandings. That the subtle differences in expression in the four preceding statements could result in so many different potential understandings suggests just how difficult it is for individuals to make themselves understood to each other. Given the potential consequences of not understanding each other, however, reasoning and rhetoric are worth our careful study and deliberate use. Reasoning is our best means of getting others to understand us and, from there, be able to engage in common purposes with us. And, very often, expressions provide a starting point for such shared reasoning.

Narratives

Narratives also provide starting points for reasoning, and—like observations and expressions—their power is elemental. Narratives come in various sizes—mini, medium, and master. Some narrative theorists have argued that all human knowing is narrative because we exist in time; others have argued that narrative knowing is misleading. Let's see what you think.

In his *Rhetoric,* Aristotle claimed that there are only two fundamental structures of persuasion (both of which should be familiar to you if you have been paying attention). The first is the enthymeme, which has the structure of claim and support with missing premises. The second is the paradigm or example, which can be understood as a miniature or highly compressed narrative.

My nephew Kurt is an example of a good boy because he has done things that good boys do so often: picked up his room; taken care of his grandmother; seen that Sarge, his cat, is safely in the house. Each of these examples unfolds a potential narrative, the story of the time Kurt did so-and-so. But examples can be understood as working by statement and proof, as well. An example is a particular instance of something more general; that is to say, an example has to be an example of something. Without the general claim *Kurt is a good boy,* Kurt's various particular deeds would not serve as examples. Regardless of the particular path it takes, however, the power of narrative in reasoning—about the past, the present, or the future—is undeniable.

Think for a moment of a film, play, television show, or book that so held your attention that you could not bear to leave the unfolding drama. What was going to happen? The compelling structure of beginning, middle, and end has long been understood as an elemental way of understanding experience and as a persuasive form of using language. Narratives are conjectural because they result from the juxtaposition—the mental putting-together—of events in the form of beginning, middle, and end. We perceive one thing as having happened, and then another thing happens, and then another and another. It is human perception that shapes events into narratives, for better or worse.

Back to the police log:

> A Lincoln St. man called police after witnessing kids rip the screen off a door at Meadow Lane; police spoke to the owner of the residence in question, who said that some kids had come over and were arguing, and damaged her door out of frustration; she said she did not want to press charges because her daughter was partly to blame.

This series shows how conjectural claims can be put together to form a narrative. The narrative certainly does not include every incident that occurred during the time the narrative covers. Instead, narratives are the result, again, of human choices of perception, memory, and expression.

Individual events can offer support for generalizations, just as individual examples can lead to general conclusions through induction. The final conjectural claim in this series—"She said she did not want to press charges because her daughter was partly to blame"—suggests how conjecture and cause are related: *What happened?* and *How did it happen?* are closely related questions. We will save our discussion of the intimate connection between conjecture and cause for Chapter 5, when we discuss causal claims at length.

The power of narratives comes from human powers of reasoning—specifically, induction, deduction, and what Wayne Booth calls **coduction,** a combination of induction and deduction that humans use in the process of narrative knowing, remembering, and judging (*The Company We Keep*, 1988). Building on a rhetorician's sense that induction and deduction rarely operate independently of one another, coduction describes the process of reasoning from general principles and from particular experiences at the same time. Events, observations, and expressions can be understood as forming patterns; narrative knowing arranges events, observations, and expressions in the form of beginning, middle, and end.

We understand our own lives and those of others very often in terms of beginning, middle, and end. An individual narrative can also take the form of telling your own story or someone else's—that is, putting together a series of anecdotes that accrue into an autobiography or a biography—formal or not. Think of the stories you tell about people to explain them to others:

> That's Gilberto; he moved here from Wichita Falls after his family won the lottery.

As though that explains everything about Gil. These narrative ways of knowing are so prevalent that they often escape our attention.

Many people who believe in God or Allah or another supreme being carry with them master narratives that what happens to them is according to the will of an omniscient force. People who rely on, for instance, Freudian analysis understand individual motives as proceeding from unresolved psychosexual narrative conflicts in early life. Capitalists believe in the narrative of the free market; socialists believe in the narrative of the emancipation of the working class. Sometimes called *master narratives,* these cultural narratives are among the largest and thus the most difficult to see. Yet they form the basis for much internal and external reasoning, particularly implicit support for claims and for the reasons that support those claims. Similarly, groups of people often have narratives about other groups they are unfamiliar with. These kinds of narratives can ossify into cultural stereotypes that lead to paths of misunderstanding and mistrust.

Another kind of very large narrative is history. Have you ever thought of history as narratival or conjectural before? One history that was well known for several centuries was Edward Gibbon's *Decline and Fall of the Roman Empire,* a multivolume history that argued for Gibbon's view of what happened to the promise of the Roman Empire. Written in the middle decades of the eighteenth century, the history reflects the values of Gibbon's time: a rationalistic questioning of early Christianity and a love of empire.

Histories—whether sweeping, like Gibbon's, or local, like the histories some of my students write about their families and their hometowns—address both conjectural questions: They tell what happened and also construct a sharable reality. Cicero—a Roman poet, politician, and rhetorician who lived just before the time of Jesus Christ—argued that it is the role of citizen writers and speakers (he used the word *orators*) to construct shared histories so that communities can understand their pasts and deliberate their futures. In Book II of Cicero's "On the Character of the Orator," one of his characters asks:

> By what other voice than that of the orator is history—the evidence of time, the light of truth, the life of memory, the directress of life, the herald of antiquity—committed to immortality? Do you see how far the study of history is the business of the orator?

Histories, narratives of what happened, cannot exist without shared reasoning in language.

In addition to mini narratives and master narratives, anecdotes are medium-sized narratives; they, too, operate conjecturally to get reasoning started or to support claims in the process of reasoning. Anecdotes function in reasoning in various ways. First, they often function as a means of identification:

> Let me tell you about the time my niece Sara caught the catfish. It was so incredible. . . .

Anecdotes function as a means of telling what happened and creating with other reasoners a sense of shared reality. If the story is told convincingly, reasoners can share a world in which Sara caught the catfish.

Anecdotes have other functions in reasoning, as well. The earliest rhetoricians noticed this and encouraged their students to write *fables*, anecdotes or stories that were illustrative of some shared principle. Aesop's fables are examples of such anecdotes, stories that reveal a value or preference or even a maxim:

> And the moral of the story is: Eat your vegetables.

Constructing hypothetical examples to support various kinds of claims is much like writing fables or constructing anecdotes about past experiences. Like other conjectures, such medium-sized narratives are powerful in reasoning and require practice to be used effectively.

Just as an example illustrates some general principle, an anecdote reveals some value. An anecdote is a moment from the past—or from the imagination—that is recalled through memory to speak to the current situation. It takes a happening from chronological time, what the Greeks called **kronos,** and puts it to use for present circumstances at the best moment, what the Greeks called **kairos**—the opportune moment. Whereas kronos or chronological time is a line,

kairos is a point on that line—

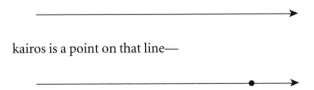

a point at which the reasoner knows, through practiced judgment, that the example or anecdote will be most effective.

❖ *Reasoning Practice*

Read the following examples of practical reasoning, and consider the questions after each. Your instructor will tell you whether to write about these questions outside class or to prepare to discuss them in class *and* whether to do so by yourself or with reasoning partners.

1. The final item in the July 15, 1999, police log:

   At 11:36 p.m. someone reported a person in the middle of Still-water Ave. yelling; the subject was gone by the time police arrived.

   • What happened?
   • How might you verify what happened?
   • What shared reality can be said to exist?
   • Where might reasoning go from here?

2. Find the conjectures in this paragraph, written by Michael Corcoran and published in the *Austin American-Statesman* (August 19, 1999):

   The sports that matter are the ones that work best on TV, the kingdom of spectatorship. That TV has become the reality became apparent when I attended my very first pro football game, which happened to be Super Bowl XXVII at the end of the '92 season. As I sat in the end zone at the Rose Bowl and watched the Cowboys pummel the Buffalo Bills, it seemed like something was missing— oh, yeah, the close-ups, the replays, the analysis, the graphics. My job was to cover Michael Jackson's halftime show, so I went to the press room at the start of the third quarter to file my story and I never returned to my seat. The game was better on TV. In person, a nine-yard run and a two-yard gain look identical. It's always 1–2–3 dogpile.

   After you've found the conjectures, make a list of possible topoi that the paragraph generates. Finally, use one conjecture in the paragraph to generate a claim at each stasis: conjecture, definition, cause, value, and procedure.

3. Here is an example of epideictic discourse, written by Franklin LaCava and published in the *Uniontown (PA) Herald–Standard* (August 16, 1998). Read it, find the conjectures, and notice whether they function as claims or as support for claims:

Shortly after Walter Spears passed away, a brief letter arrived from a New Jersey couple I've known for years.

Enclosed was a clipping from the *New York Times,* showing this year's wagon train making its way down the National Pike.

Immediately, I scanned the photo for Walter, but couldn't pick him out in the crunch of wagons, animals, and dust.

Pity, it seemed, that the labor of love he had so faithfully championed for 25 years had "made the big time" in the last year he would participate, but his efforts would get no special notice.

Of course, a vain thought like this would have been quickly brushed away with a snort of brusque laughter by Walt Spears.

Anyone lucky enough to have spent some time with him and his wife, Cloe, during those late May days when the canvas-covered wagons command our attention would know that personal recognition and glory were the farthest thoughts from their minds.

Before he stepped down as wagonmaster, he offered me his philosophy in a single sentence: "If one man's got trouble, the whole thing's got trouble until the thing gets going again."

In other words, if somebody was sick or a wheel or axle was broken, no one was abandoned. The train simply stopped until the problem was dealt with.

The period of America's moving frontier is all but lost in myth and cliche, probably the result of too many Western movies, romantic claptrap and mind-numbing episodes of "Death Valley Days."

But the wagon train is a real event, so Walter believed that he had, through personal experience, found the essence of community spirit on the frontier.

The frontier sense of community had to have come from the sense of common purpose on the way west. Quite simply, America's pioneers did not have many options—the saying went that you married the person you sat next to on the wagon. People's lives depended on cooperation, so customs were established as they settled.

Call it the pioneer spirit or what you will, the wagonmaster's sense of the common good evolved into a primitive civic code.

Spears had lived for some 45 years in Hopwood, though the family roots were in Markleysburg, near the intersection of the Mason-Dixon line bordering Pennsylvania, Maryland and West Virginia.

"I was 20 years old before I knew if I was a Rebel or a Yankee," he often joked.

My last memory of Walter Spears is perhaps the best.

It was a picture-perfect spring day, as this year's wagon train—the longest ever—rolled into Brownsville.

Near the bend leading to Nemacolin Castle, 87-year-old Walter Spears leaped from his buckboard and vociferously directed the horses around the bend.

The little broad-shouldered man in the buckskin coat and dark slouch hat was directing things in a way that only a lifetime of tending animals could instill.

The day was like the photo from the *New York Times*—clear and bright.

The wagon train was like the picture—long and colorful.

As for finding Walter Spears in the photo, it finally occurred to me: He was everywhere.

4

Definitions

They Can Change Everything

Rhetoric and Definitions

Imagine two people in a building. (Have you imagined this before?) One of them says, "It's hailing." The other one says, "No it's not; I can't hear it." They both go outside and see whether it is hailing.

As you might recall, this hypothetical example suggests that a fact is a fact when two or more individuals agree on the conjecture in question. A conjecture is a fact to the extent that it has been verified. (We have been through that.)

Then imagine that one of the people says, "It's not hailing. Actually, it's sleeting." The stasis has just shifted from **conjecture** to **definition.** If their reasoning is going to get anywhere, the two will need to talk about their different **definitional criteria** for hail and sleet—size? mass? atomic structure?

Although I am sure you know what a definition is, you might not know that arguing with and about definitions is another fundamental element of reasoning. Knowing when you need to stop and define something during the process of reasoning—and knowing what kinds of definitional arguments different reasoning situations require—is central to being an effective practical reasoner. This chapter will discuss some common types and functions of claims at the stasis of definition. In addition, we will briefly consider some of the problems of definition—how the act of defining is always deeply rhetorical. First, however, let's look at one more example of definitional reasoning.

After Minnesota Governor Jesse Ventura, a former professional wrestler, announced that he had agreed to serve as referee for a professional boxing match, National Public Radio's Noah Adams interviewed Lou Fez, former undisputed world-champion professional wrestler from Norfolk, Virginia, to see what Fez thought about Ventura's decision to reenter the ring. Fez, as Adams pointed out, was a professional wrestler "when Jesse Ventura was in diapers."

However, Fez was not particularly interested in arguing about the value of what Ventura was doing. Rather than arguing at the stasis of *value*, Fez wanted to argue about the *definition* of wrestling: "What you see on television today is not wrestling," Fez said. "It is choreographed tumbling."

He returned to his point several times during the interview: "That's what I'm trying to say: That is not wrestling. You can watch those matches for five or ten minutes and not see one wrestling move." Fez defined wrestling as a sport that has certain moves and to which men devoted their lives. Wrestling, for Fez, was a vocation, not merely a big-money spectacle.

As we discussed in Chapter 1, a critical problem with practical reasoning today is that too many arguers rush to the stases of value and procedure—Are you for it or against it?—rather than carefully and patiently taking the time to deliberate about definitions. Like conjectures, definitional claims only rarely encompass entire arguments. However, again, like conjectures, definitions are often the foundations on which arguments at other stases are constructed.

Let's push these metaphorical definitions of *definition* a bit further—or add two more metaphors to the mix. Whereas conjectures might be understood as the soil in which arguments take root, definitions are the direction finders. Definitions make fundamental differences in the paths reasoning can go:

Is AIDS a civil rights issue or a public health issue?

Those two definitions each lead down very different paths of reasoning.

Is a person's salvation defined by grace or by good works?

That definitional distinction was at the heart of the Christian Reformation.

Are college sports a central part of undergraduate education for student-athletes or just another means for universities to raise money and attract publicity?

Is a cheerleader an ornament or an athlete?

And so on. Definitional moves are **logotropic** in that they can turn (trope) an argument (logos) from one path to another very quickly.

Definitions, then, are not just the meanings of words we look up in dictionaries. Definitions are kinds of arguments, and they have serious consequences for the direction as well as the destination of any practical reasoning.

Dictionary Definitions

Definitions are not established in heaven—as far as I know. Instead, definitions are created by communities of people. The definitions that we find in dictionaries are records of the meanings that groups of people have assigned to certain words in their language. Many words have several meanings recorded in the dictionary. Some of those meanings are recognized only by people living in a particular region, others only by people in certain cultures or subcultures, and others only by people in certain professions. And many definitions never get into dictionaries at all. What is called *soda* in eastern Pennsylvania is called *pop* in western Pennsylvania; "my pop has gone flat" might sound like a tragedy to someone who did not know the difference.

Time can also change definitions: Words may acquire new meanings or may lose meanings they once had. My favorite example of this is *toilet water,* which is not what you might think. *Toilet water* is a kind of fragrance, and its name reflects the fact that *toilet* used to refer to the whole routine of cleansing the body and readying it for presentation. *Doing one's toilet* meant bathing and combing and powdering and, yes, putting on some kind of pleasant-smelling concoction. *Toilet water* as fragrance thus resulted from a broadening of the French word *toilette,* the cloth cover of a dressing table. So now you know.

If the meaning of a word in the dictionary is labeled **archaic,** it was once recognized and accepted by groups of people but generally is not any longer. If a new meaning or an archaic meaning were proposed as the basis for an argument, the reasoning parties would have to agree to accept that meaning in their discussion.

Neologisms

Not all words—and not all meanings, of course—make it into every dictionary. A word used quite often by television journalists after the death of John F. Kennedy, Jr.—*cremains,* meaning "cremated remains"—is in no standard desk dictionary that I could find. Likewise, *cafetorium*—the combination cafeteria and auditorium that many public schools now have—is not in any dictionary I could find. Yet these words not only exist, they allow us to make conjectures about our shared world: That a rhyming slang word came to be used on national television perhaps suggests how common cremation has become. That school districts would have to consolidate rooms for eating with rooms for public assemblies may suggest how short of resources public schools have become.

Sometimes called **neologisms** or **coined words,** new words (or new meanings for old words) can be very persuasive—largely because of their relative shock value. However, they rarely become the foundations for entire arguments. Instead, like *logotropic* above, neologisms are ways of making concepts easier to perceive and remember.

Stipulative Definitions

While some arguments turn, or trope, on definitions that are quoted from dictionaries or are coined, other arguments may be based on what are called **stipulative definitions,** or definitions that a particular individual or group has formulated for the purposes of a particular reasoning problem. The definition might be identical with or similar to one or another of a word's dictionary definitions, but it might be quite different. A stipulative definition represents someone's tentative view of the nature of something for the purposes of a particular reasoning problem.

A stipulative definition will work in an argument if the reasoner can get others to accept the definition—accept it for at least the time being, for the moment of **kairos**—for the purposes of the discussion at hand. Another way to put it is to say that a stipulative definition is a *working definition.* The reasoners might agree to accept—at least tentatively—a definition of some key term or concept simply to make it possible for the discussion or argument to go forward. Sometimes the parties involved will settle on a stipulative definition because it is more pertinent than dictionary definitions to the context in which the reasoning is taking place.

One advantage of a stipulative definition is that it informs everyone involved in the discussion or argument what a particular key term means in a particular context. One of the parties says, "Here is what I mean when I use the term *wrestling:* . . ." There is a certain straight-forwardness about such an explicit designation of meaning. It allows shared reasoning to proceed because the terms are open to scrutiny. Explicit stipulative definitions invite the assent of those reasoning together as the reasoning process proceeds.

Some people, on the other hand, adopt a stipulative definition in a particular discussion, but they never reveal explicitly what that definition is. They have their own view of what a key term means, but they do not open that definition to scrutiny by making it explicit. In effect, they are seeking to win acceptance by unreflective or deceptive means. Advertising often works this way, as do so-called invitations to sign up for credit cards.

But I can think of no better—or worse—example of deception by stipulative definition than President Clinton's infamous attempt to destabilize a very familiar word—*is*—in one of his depositions before his 1999 impeachment: "It depends on what your definition of *is* is," the president said. Forced through questions to make his stipulative definition of *is* explicit, the president was unable to sustain his reasoning. Clinton's deception at the stasis of definition also suggests the closeness of the link between arguments at the stasis of definition and arguments at the stasis of value; that his definition of *is* might have met legal criteria does not mean that it necessarily would meet moral or ethical criteria, as well. Definitions and evaluations both are arguments about the nature of a thing, a point we will return to in Chapter 6.

Specific Means of Defining

So, definitional claims can turn entire arguments. But after a definitional path has been chosen, by what means can reasoners support their definitional claims?

Synonym

Perhaps the simplest and most common way of defining a concept or thing is to give synonyms for it. Take the familiar word *companion,* for instance. Even without resorting to a dictionary or a thesaurus, most of us could cite several synonyms for this word: *friend, comrade, associate, colleague, mate, fellow, confidant, pal.* Of course, such alternative words are only relatively synonymous; each word has different shades of meaning, or connotations. Of the synonyms above, *associate* is probably closest in denotative meaning to *companion; confidant* and *pal* are probably the farthest. The point is that in resorting to synonyms to give others some idea of what a term means, we have to be aware of the shades of interchangeability of the synonyms. Like similes, another means of defining by similarity that we will discuss below, synonyms are only more or less like the word that is being defined.

Indeed, the words we use to define our relationships show how slippery synonyms can be. What kinds of differences are suggested if you introduce someone as your *friend,* your *girlfriend,* your *intended,* your *partner,* your *steady,* or your *lover?* If you choose to marry, what is the difference between having a *husband* and having a *spouse?* A *partner* or a *wife?* And what relationships are allowed to be defined as *marriages?* Sometimes it seems our language has relatively few words for describing human relationships. In any case, while synonyms are means of defining, they are certainly not ways of necessarily limiting the connotations of whatever it is you are reasoning about at the stasis of definition. Synonyms can raise as many questions as they can answer.

Etymology

We may sometimes choose to define a term by giving its etymology—not to be confused with entomology, which is the study of bugs. **Etymology,** or the study of the historical derivation of a word from its earliest form, enables reasoners to be more precise in their use of particular words or to appreciate rich but submerged senses of a particular word. The word *companion,* for instance, derives from the Latin *cum,* meaning "with," and *panis,* meaning "bread." Tracing *companion* back through its literal derivation from Latin suggests that a companion is someone with whom one has shared food, or broken bread—one of the closest relationships one could have with another.

When we reason using the derivation of a word, we can give others a more profound sense of the historical resonance of a word. It is wise to remember, however, that language is always changing: Words have a tendency to drift far from their root meanings. Therefore, words today often have meanings far removed from their original meanings. The word *villain* derives from the Late Latin word *villanus,* which meant "a farm servant." There is little if any trace of that meaning in the word *villain* today.

Description

Another way of defining something is to give an extended description of it. Dictionaries give succinct definitions of words designating persons, places, things, and concepts. But sometimes we need more fully developed **descriptions** of things to persuade our reasoning companions of what it is that we are trying to define.

For instance, if we wanted to explain to a younger sibling the registration process at a university, we might cite a definition from the student handbook: "the process by which students enroll for classes." But this brief definition might not be very helpful to students registering for the first time at a university. So we might have to reason further, putting together a very detailed description of the process:

> First you make sure the following forms have been filed; then you call a particular phone number, making sure you have the necessary information. Then you need to go to the registrar's office on campus and wait in a long line. Finally, someone in the registrar's office gives you a piece of blue paper that lists all your classes. That's how you know when you are registered.

It is good to note that—in giving developed descriptions of things, concepts, and processes—reasoners might use anecdotes, examples, and analogies. The medieval *exemplum* was a narrative intended to illustrate or support a moral lesson, as we discussed in Chapter 3. Practical reasoners frequently resort to extended descriptions in order to elucidate an idea, thing, concept, or process. Consider this book, for instance.

Analysis

Defining by analyzing involves taking a thing or concept and dividing it into all of its parts. For instance, if you were to define by **analysis** a *human life*, you might break it into the following parts: *birth, childhood, adolescence, adulthood, middle age, advanced age,* and *death.* Or if you were defining by analysis a *football team,* you would name all of the positions (*fullback, linebacker,* etc.) and then describe them, one after the other.

In addition to helping you define something in the process of reasoning, defining by analysis can provide a means of organizing or arranging your reasoning on a larger scale. Imagine reasoning through each of the parts of something—the elements of the public debate over health care or the process of installing a drought-resistant lawn—and proceeding through each part, one after another, in the order you judge to be best. Analysis is a powerful reasoning tool.

Classification

In 1981, when the Reagan administration urged school lunch programs to classify ketchup as a vegetable, not everyone was willing to assent to that definitional reasoning. To classify an idea or thing is to place it into a category and to suggest that it shares a certain essence with the other things in that category.

The easiest way to understand **classification** is to think biologically: An organism's **genus** is the group that it can be said to belong to when its structure or development suggests it is related to other organisms. And an organism's **species** is what sets it apart, by one criterion or another, from the other organisms in a group. The species of roses—tea roses, climbing roses, shrub roses—together constitute the genus *Rosa.* The species horses and zebras are in the genus *Equus.* This kind of classification is sometimes called **genus/difference,** and its origins are in Plato's dialogical method and in the work of his student Aristotle, though the process of scientific classification was perfected in the eighteenth century by Carolus Linnaeus.

Just as dictionary definitions do not come from heaven, Linnaeus admitted that his system of grouping plants and animals by structure and form was not absolute. Only recently, however, has his system faced serious challenge, and the challenge points again to the centrality of reasoning and argument to any branch of human knowledge and action, including science.

For the past several years, some botanists have been trying to change the foundation for plant classification from structure to genetic makeup. As Brent Mishler, a professor at the University of California, Berkeley, said on the radio show *Sounds Like Science:*

> One of the things we're emphasizing . . . is that *plant* itself is no longer a good word. You can't divide the complex multicellular organisms into plants and animals, as is traditionally done.

It turns out that the organisms biologists call *plants*—green plants, kelps, algae and fungi—are not directly related to one another genetically. So, arguably, they do not belong in the same group because they do not share the same essence.

Classifying something by common essence is also sometimes called **essential definition.** The formula for this kind of definition is as follows:

Term being defined + linking verb + genus + difference

An example of this would be as follows:

> An automobile is a vehicle that has four wheels and is propelled by an internal-combustion engine.

In this example, *automobile* is the thing or the term being defined. The linking verb is *is*. *Vehicle* is the genus or general class into which an automobile can be put. And the rest of the definition is the difference, that is, what distinguishes an automobile from other vehicles—bicycles, motorcycles, carts, wagons, snowmobiles, skateboards.

An essential definition puts the thing to be defined into a general class and then gives some details that distinguish the thing from other things in its class.

The Negative

Another powerful way of defining something is to say what it is *not:*

> A cheerleader is not an ornament; rather, a cheerleader is an athlete.
>
> Free speech is not a luxury; it is a right.
>
> Graffiti is not a crime; it is an art.

And so on. See how definition by the negative depends on the same kind of classification that essential definitions do? In fact, another way of understanding negative definitions is by seeing them as arguments about the absence of a particular essence.

Defining something by a negative is particularly effective in practical reasoning if you are trying to change your listeners' or readers' minds about what a term means. If someone already has a notion of what, say, *democracy* means, starting with that definition ("You might think that democracy is a system of government in which all people share power") and making it the basis of your negative definition is a reasonable way to proceed toward a different definition. It begins with what is already in your readers' or listeners' minds and thus begins with identification.

Metaphor and Simile

In Chapter 3, we discussed conjectures that take the form of analogies, metaphors, and similes. These are often definitional in effect, and so they deserve some attention in this chapter, as well. In addition, like classifications and essential definitions, metaphors and similes raise profound questions about the nature of naming and definition in general.

Metaphors claim that one thing or idea is *identical* to another thing or idea. Song lyrics are one means of pointing out the power—and instability—of metaphors. Consider this line:

> Love is a rose, but you better not pick it; it only grows when it's on the vine.

Now, consider what is done to the metaphor when a bit of immature rhyming takes over:

> Love is a nose, but you better not . . .

Silly, I know. Still, the metaphor's power is in the implied identity of—and hence comparison between—two things or ideas which, in fact, are different. Metaphor is particularly likely to function definitionally when it operates, as Aristotle first pointed out, from the better-known thing to the lesser-known thing. Did you know *roses* and *noses* before you knew *love?*

The whole idea of metaphor—as you will recall from our discussion of conjecture—necessitates a shared reality. As rhetorician Richard Lanham points out, that is both the power of and the danger of metaphor:

> Perhaps it is metaphor's intrinsic *instability* which has attracted so much recent attention: to appreciate the metaphoricity of a metaphor we must posit a nonmetaphorical, normative "reality" against which to project the metaphorical transformation. (*Handlist of Rhetorical Terms*, 1991)

This suggests in yet another way how fundamental conjecture is to all reasoning. Without a basis of shared reality—of identification, gained by reasoning in language—no external reasoning can proceed.

Writing for listeners and readers in Amherst, Massachusetts, in the 1930s, poet Robert Frost also wanted to communicate the power and danger of metaphor. Let's listen to him talk about a common metaphorical expression that has lost its metaphorical echo for many of us:

> Another metaphor that has interested us in our time and has done all our thinking for us is the metaphor of evolution. Never mind going into the Latin word. The metaphor is simply the metaphor of the growing plant or of the growing thing. And somebody, very brilliantly, quite a while ago, said that the whole universe, the whole of everything, was like unto a growing thing. That is all. I know the metaphor will break down at some point, but it has not failed everywhere. It is a very brilliant metaphor, I acknowledge, though I myself get too tired of the kind of essay that talks about the evolution of candy, say, or the evolution of elevators—the evolution of this, that, and the other. Everything is evolution. . . .
>
> What I am pointing out is that unless you are at home in the metaphor, unless you have had your proper poetical education in the metaphor, you are not safe anywhere. Because you are not at ease with figurative values: you don't know the metaphor in its strength and its weakness.

I was reminded of Frost's words about the metaphor of evolution when I heard one author recently describe the stock market as *being in its adolescence* and another describe the World Wide Web as being *in its infancy*. How valid is the author's move of identifying a stage in an economic or technological entity with a stage in a human life? But *adolescence* itself is a category that came out of a certain period of time and a certain theory of human development, so who is to say that the stock market cannot have an adolescence? And what does it mean if it can? What can we infer about the market's *adulthood*?

Whereas definitional reasoning by metaphor suggests identity between the things being compared, **simile** suggests only *likeness*. "Writing is so hard," wrote Scott Blackwood, the coordinator of my university's Undergraduate Writing Center, recently in a memo. "It's like hitting a 100-mile-per-hour fastball on a chilly night in October." Scott was not saying writing is identical to hitting that fastball; he was saying that writing is *like* that, similar to that. And he chose a figurative definition in order to get his readers to think about what he was defining in a new way—and to get them to appreciate how difficult it is to do well.

A definitional argument is rarely settled for long. That is why reasoning at the stasis of definition is so powerful. It can change the path and destination of reasoning, and its methods are powerful for arranging as well as inventing shared discourses. Definitions can change everything.

❖ *Reasoning Practice*

1. Consider the word *logorrhea*.

   - Using only your own internal reasoning, write down five possible definitions of this word.

   - Then, ask a few other people what they think the word means, and write down their guesses.

   - Finally, find a dictionary that has the word *logorrhea* in it. Compare the definitions you and others invented, and consider what factors make a definition correct or incorrect.

2. Chris Riemenschneider, a music reviewer for the *Austin American-Statesman*, wrote in the July 21, 1999, edition about the commercial

success of Lilith Fair and how it is changing conventional wisdom about the music business:

> Before Lilith, having two women on the same concert marquee or even during the same hour of pop radio was considered dangerous, like drinking beer before liquor or putting ketchup on the same side of the burger as mustard.
>
> Now, music-biz thinkers who watched Lilith gross $44 million its first two summers have realized it all goes down the same tube.

What definitional claims do you find here? How are they supported? What is Riemenschneider saying is identical and/or similar to what?

3. How does the writer of the following posting to an academic-professional listserv support the definition of *sexual harassment*?

CRTNET NEWS
September 13, 1999, Number 4369
Communication Research and Theory Network
a service of the National Communication Association
Date: Fri 9/10/99 6:48 PM
From: Erica Michaels Hollander
Re: Unwanted sexual attention and harassment

As a lawyer who has tried a fair number of sex discrimination and harassment cases in twenty plus years of practice and a doctoral student in Human Communication, I have been fascinated by this discussion of sexual harassment and the different senses in which the same words are used in the different contexts. What is actionable at law is what case law defines as sexual harassment, first recognized by the U.S. Supreme Court in 1986 as a brand of sexual discrimination of a more subtle sort in which the atmosphere of the workplace is tainted by abuses of power. The term originated, so far as I know, when aggrieved victims of outrageous acts in the workplace successfully pled that sexual discrimination in terms of direct adverse consequences of supervisory decision making based on gender preferences for promotions, perks, layoffs, etc. were insufficient to cover all the serious and more subtle harms that might befall one not a member of the preferred group. See *Vinson v. Meritor Savings Bank*, 477 U.S. 57 (1986). It has since very rarely been recognized by courts in situations outside superior-subordinate because it began with the idea of egregious abuse of power in the workplace to extract sexual favors or impose unwanted advances on one essentially held captive by the need to earn a living. Expansive thinking by some human relations departments and a few courts around the country has led some to talk of customer harassment of vulnerable employees (like cocktail servers) and coworker-peer (where no protection is offered by the boss, e.g.) harassment, but the idea of an extension wholesale of harassment doctrine to the schools such that teachers can readily prove students have harassed them is far from likely under the law as it exists today. It may be useful to look back to the facts of the case that convinced the Supreme Court to recognize sexual harassment in the first instance to get a feeling for where the law is on the matter not 15 yrs later: that case arose from repeated and unwanted sexual intercourse between a bank worker and supervisor on which promotion and job success depended.

We have not moved all that far from that kind of idea in case law since then, even if many who feel they have been the recipients of unwanted sexual attention or intimidation in the university or elsewhere think we should have.

Erica Michaels Hollander, Esq.
University of Denver Department of Human Communication Studies

4. Can you libel a vegetable? Write a paragraph defending that definitional use of *libel*, and then find a source in a newspaper or magazine that either supports or refutes your view.

5

Causes and Consequences

A Sense of How the World Works

How Could This Happen?

On September 15, 1999, at 7 p.m., The University of Texas at Austin officially reopened the observation deck of its campus bell tower. The observation deck had been closed more than 20 years earlier in the wake of several suicides over four decades and after a student ascended the tower in 1966 with a footlocker of guns and ammunition and opened fire, killing 14 people and injuring more than 30 during a roughly 90-minute rampage.

At nearly the same moment as the university was celebrating the reopening of the observation deck with music and fireworks, less than 200 miles north, an armed man walked into a church and opened fire, killing 7 people and wounding 7 more. Then he pointed the gun at his head and pulled the trigger, killing himself.

How could these things have happened?

Reasoning about how or why something came to be is reasoning at the stasis of **cause.** As we discussed in Chapter 3, conjecture and cause are intimately related. Like conjecture, causal reasoning involves putting together in language an account of what happened. In inventing a causal account, narrative is often involved—first, this happened; then, this happened; finally, this happened—again suggesting how closely connected are conjecture and cause. While conjectures answer the question *What happened?* or *Does a shared reality exist?* causal reasoning attempts to answer this question: *How did it come to happen?* As a result, causal reasoning is even more complicated than definitional or even conjectural reasoning. In fact, it is fair to say that causal reasoning is the most difficult kind of reasoning.

Causal reasoning has connections to other stases, as well. If a particular effect has consistently negative or positive consequences, causal reasoning can lead to reasoning at the stasis of value, which is our topic in Chapter 6. And if we want to try to make a certain effect happen again—or try to prevent a certain effect from ever happening again—reasoning about causes and effects can be a central component in larger arguments at the stasis of procedure, which we will discuss in Chapter 7.

Causal reasoning comes in many, many forms—not just the spectacularly tragic:

How did the porch swing get broken?

How did I not see that deer dart out in front of my car?

Is plastic wrap dangerous to your health?

How did my friend know I was just about to call him when he e-mailed me?

Can eating broccoli prevent cancer?

How do video games change the children who play them?

Can music calm the savage beast?

How did we get here?

Causal reasoning usually brings with it some larger sense of how the world works. Some people pray or meditate because they believe in a causal link between those activities and certain effects—even if the effect is just strengthening the habit of prayer or meditation. Some people build up the soil in their gardens because they have learned that healthy soil helps seeds germinate and plants thrive. Some people exercise because they know it makes them healthier—but not all of us exercise as often as we should: I wonder why.

The territory of causal reasoning is as wide as the distance between folk remedies and science, between creationism and evolution, between sex education and stories about storks. Causal reasoning is something we do, whether we are aware of it or not. This chapter endeavors to help you see how common causal reasoning is—as well as to encourage you to reflect on the premises that stand behind your own views of causality. You are reading this book for a reason, right? What causality stands behind that?

Conjecture, then, answers *What happened?* Definition answers *What should we call it?* And cause answers *How did it come to happen?* or *Why did it happen?* Answering the *How?* or *Why?* question involves us in trying to persuade others that our hypothesis about why something happened is plausible, if not incontrovertible. Causal reasoning, like other kinds of human reasoning, concerns that which can be otherwise—that which is probable but not certain.

Reasoning from Effect to Cause

One of the most common instances of cause-and-effect reasoning is the mystery novel or detective story. It often begins with the discovery of a dead body. The natural question to ask upon such a discovery is:

How or why did the body that lies before us come to be lifeless?

If a quick examination of the corpse makes it obvious that the deceased did not die from natural causes, the subsequent series of questions includes:

Who did it?

How was it done?

Why was it done?

Answering these questions involves the detective in a chain of cause-and-effect reasoning. If you have read mystery novels, you know they often end with the detective gathering the family and friends of the deceased in the library, laying out the chain of reasoning that led the detective to discover who was the murderer, and explaining how and why the butler—or whomever—did it.

Detective stories work by deduction. Readers who are consistently able to figure out mysteries in novels or on television are able to single out each character and, by process of elimination, determine whether he or she is the murderer. Starting out with an effect—in this case, a corpse—and reasoning your way to a discovery of the cause—the murderer—is always captivating, at least in the pages of a novel. In life, however, causal reasoning is rarely so elegant or so clear, particularly when it concerns deliberative, rather than forensic, questions.

Reasoning from Cause to Effect

Causal reasoning works in the other direction, too—from cause to effect. When we distinguish something as a cause, it is likely that we wonder whether that cause will always produce the same effect or effects.

When we smell gas in a kitchen, for instance, we probably are fearful that it will asphyxiate those in the building or will produce an explosion—two potential effects of leaking gas. When we read on the Internet that the temperature will plummet during the night to below freezing, we worry whether the pipes will freeze in our building. When we read news reports that the Federal Reserve is planning to raise interest rates, we are afraid that we might be less likely than before to pay off our debts. When we eat a second serving of shoo-fly pie, we can expect our waistbands to be tighter. Causes and effects.

Knowing the potential and usual effects of certain causes can help us mightily in our reasoning. This knowledge may help us anticipate—and therefore avoid—the negative effects of those causes when we detect their presence. A potential effect, of course, does not invariably occur when a cause is present. And sometimes an existent cause will produce an unusual or unexpected effect; chaos theory has helped explain those kinds of phenomena. In short, the relationship between most causes and most effects—outside the laboratory—is not necessary. In reasoning about things that can be otherwise, the relationship between causes and effects is more or less probable.

Reasoning from causes to effects can also be thought of as reasoning about **consequences.** Assuming that conditions are the same as they were the last time a cause was present, the same or a similar consequence is likely to occur. As we will discuss further in the next chapter, consequences provide one way of making claims of value. That is to say, one way of reasoning about whether a thing is good or bad is by reasoning about whether its consequences are good or bad.

Antecedence-Subsequence

Reasoners need to be careful to distinguish reasoning that is based on the cause-and-effect relationship from reasoning that is based on the antecedence-subsequence relationship. The **antecedence-subsequence** relationship is deceptively similar to the cause-and-effect relationship. Antecedence-subsequence reasoning operates on the principle that when a certain condition, situation, or disposition exists, something will follow. But the something that follows—what is subsequent—is not necessarily produced by, is not necessarily caused by, what went before it—the antecedent.

For instance, when a native of the United States reaches the age of 18, he or she becomes eligible to vote. The privilege of voting *follows* the attainment of a certain age, but this privilege is *not caused by* that attainment. By legal definition, the privilege follows having reached a certain age. The attainment of age is only a matter of time; one did not cause the other.

When the water in the bird bath freezes on a cold winter morning, is this an instance of the cause-and-effect principle or the antecedence-subsequence principle? The freezing of the water certainly followed the drop in temperature. But since pure water will always freeze when the temperature slips below 32 degrees Fahrenheit (or 0 degrees Centigrade), we have to assent that the low temperature caused the freezing. In that case, it is not just a matter of time. As long as the laws of physical chemistry hold, the water will freeze.

What about the superstition that bad luck will follow if someone walks under a ladder? People can cite instances of this, yet there is no incontrovertible proof that walking under a ladder invariably or even usually will cause bad luck. Perhaps the bad luck happened by chance. In any case, it happened subsequently, not consequently.

Whether we reason from cause to effect or effect to cause, we have to be aware of certain principles that govern cause-and-effect relationships. Otherwise, we open our reasoning to easy refutation by others.

Post Hoc, Ergo Propter Hoc

Pardon my language, but *Post hoc, ergo propter hoc* is Latin for "After this, therefore because of this." The phrase is a shorthand way to describe reasoning that confuses a relationship of antecedence-subsequence with a relationship of cause and effect.

I washed the car this morning, so it rained.

Did it rain because I washed the car? Probably not, but some people are tempted to reason in that way, perhaps because they feel that they are unlucky.

I ate the clam soup and started feeling bad a few hours later.

Did the clam soup make me ill? Possibly, but it would take further reasoning to know for sure.

Human reasoning is easily seduced by *post hoc, ergo propter hoc* thinking. But remember that a temporal relationship between two events does not necessarily mean there is a causal relationship between them. Causality involves reasoning about change over time; *post hoc, ergo propter hoc* reasoning conflates time with causality.

Chance as a Causal Factor

One causal factor that is often overlooked is chance. The ancient Greeks distinguished *chance (tuke)* from *art (tekne)* and reasoned that human knowledge and informed practice could, to some extent, arm us against twists of fate and chance. Rhetoric itself was understood by Aristotle as a *tekne,* that is, a human art that empowered reasoners to overcome the caprices of chance by study, practice, and habit. Yet chance continues to be the cause of a great many effects.

Chance can quite compellingly be said to be the causal factor between the reopening of The University of Texas tower and the shootings in Forth Worth. Coincidence. Happened at the same time. Yet, like conjecture, chance tells: That is, that the two events happened at the same time offers possible topoi for invention. You have probably known people who think that nothing is a coincidence. These people are likely to interpret chance events in some meaningful way. Different cultures value chance differently, and knowing the role chance plays in your audience's or reasoning partners' enthymemes will help you figure out how to reason with them.

Chance can also provide reasoners with a consistent means of refusing to draw conclusions. In that way, cause can be understood as a fairly unproductive means of thinking about how to change a cause-and-effect relationship or of breaking a causal chain. Faced with the same effect following from the same cause, it becomes more and more difficult to attribute causality to chance.

Chance and Causality, Myth and Cosmology

Back to that building. Remember: Where it's raining?

Well, it's raining again, and the two people standing at the window watching want to know why.

As you might recall, one of the rainwatchers is a meteorologist. She explains that it is raining because the temperature and the dewpoint are the same. The other person is not a meteorologist. He says that it is raining because the benevolent gods are blessing the earth with needed moisture.

This hypothetical example is meant to reveal two fundamental world views that underlie how people are likely to understand causal reasoning. The meteorologist's perspective is **cosmological;** that is, it is based on the assumption that the world is orderly and governed by consistent rules. The other person's view is **mythopoeic;** that is, it is based on the assumption that the world is governed not by impersonal rules but by the personalities of deities. Both the cosmological and the mythopoeic views come from ancient times, and both still thrive today, as is evidenced by contemporary reasoning about the origins of the world and the origins of humans. The debate over whether and how to teach creationism and evolution, in particular, suggests that these two world views are still influential today.

Historian of philosophy W. K. C. Guthrie argued in the mid twentieth century that ancient Greek thought "progressed" from the mythopoeic view to the cosmological or *rational* view, as he called it. Yet subsequent scholarship has persuasively argued that both views have existed beside each other throughout human history. *Mythopoeic* views, again, tend to see causality as involving issues of personality—a jealous god, an angry goddess—and as revealed in stories or myths. *Cosmological* views tend to see causality as involving the laws of nature; cosmology assumes an ordered and consistent universe.

While chance has much in common with the mythopoeic view, most other forms of reasoning depend on a view of the universe as orderly and ordered. As I said earlier in the chapter, while discussing the relationship between effects and their causes, "Assuming that conditions are the same as they were the last time a cause was present, the same or a similar consequence is likely to occur." See how this kind of causal reasoning assumes an ordered universe that is consistently governed by immutable laws of nature? In the late twentieth century, chaos theory threw a bit of a wrench into the idea of an immutably ordered world, and various juries are still out on the origins of the universe. In any case, please notice that causal reasoning depends on some sense of how the world works. In order to understand other people's causal reasoning, you may need to ask them about their claims and to observe their actions in order to understand their view of how the world works.

Some Guidelines for Causal Reasoning

As this chapter has tried to suggest, reasoning about causes and effects is very tricky; therefore, such reasoning can easily fail to convince careful reasoning partners and audiences. Here are some guidelines that can help keep you from slipping into faulty causal reasoning:

- *A cause always comes before its effect.* There is no way that you can reason convincingly that a phenomenon that occurred after another phenomenon caused it. It is unreasonable to suggest that the thunder, which we always hear during or after we see lightning, caused the lightning.

- *An effect can have a number of possible causes.* For instance, if you find a broken window in your building, you cannot assume that a person broke it. Vibrations from an explosion in the neighborhood might have broken it; a large bird might have slammed into it; or some temperature change or weather event might have broken it. In supporting a claim about how the window got broken, you have to eliminate all other possible causes if you want to be as persuasive as possible.

- *The cause we assign to an effect must be capable of producing that effect.* In other words, the alleged cause must be an adequate cause. The frail, arthritic gardener could hardly be suspected of having strangled the tall, robust, athletic butler. But the gardener's son, who has won several medals for his weight lifting, should be questioned by the detectives.

- *We must consider whether the hypothetical cause always produces the effect that it is capable of producing and whether it invariably produces the same effect.* In other words, we must establish that a putative cause not only could but also would produce a particular effect. Lightning is capable of starting a forest fire, but lightning does not invariably start a fire whenever it strikes. So until we can establish conclusively that lightning started the fire in the national forest, we will have to consider other possible causes. Maybe the campers who left the park hastily set the fire, either deliberately or carelessly.

- *If something occurs repeatedly, the most likely cause is the one that all the occurrences have in common.* This principle is John Stuart Mill's *Method of Agreement.* If several people who ate at separate tables in a restaurant on the same evening got sick within a few hours, they may have suffered from food poisoning. The most likely cause for their sickness is the item on the menu that they all ate that night. Suppose an interview with the stricken patrons reveals that all of them ate roasted chicken, one of the specials that evening. The fact that chicken is easily contaminated adds to the likelihood that it may be the cause of the problem.

- *If an effect occurs in some situations but not others, the cause may be the single thing that is different between the similar situations.* This principle is Mill's *Method of Difference.* Let's say two neighbors divided up the tomato plants they bought on sale at a local nursery. The following August, Lucinda harvested a bountiful crop of big, juicy, vine-ripened tomatoes, but Jack's tomatoes were small and blighted at the blossom end. Lucinda and Jack certainly did many of the same things in planting and caring for their tomato plants. But they did one thing differently, and that single difference accounted for the unequal harvests: Blossom end rot is caused by lack of watering, so Lucinda was not surprised to learn that Jack had not watered his tomatoes during the hot, dry months of June and July.

- *If a particular situation increases or decreases, you must find a plausible cause that acts in a similar or inverse fashion.* That is, you need to find a cause that increases or decreases as the effect increases—or that decreases as the effect increases or decreases or increases as the effect decreases. Got that? This principle comes from Mill's *Method of Concomitant Variation.* Suppose that you wanted to reason about the cause of an increase in vandalism by teenagers in your community. Of course, there could be a number of causes for that increase. First of all, you have to search for plausible causes for the increase—that is, there is probably a fairly obvious or reasonable connection between the cause and the effect. Once you have found some plausible causes, you must examine the correlation between the various causes and the effect. If some of the possible causes and the effect do not interact either proportionately or inversely, those causes are probably not operating solely in this situation.

A persistent rise in the stock markets, for instance, does not seem to be a plausible cause for a rise of teenage vandalism in your community. (By examining a chain of causes, however, you might be able to make a case for such a cause-and-effect relationship.) But if there has been a significant rise or decline in the population of teenagers in the community recently, that may provide a plausible cause. Further, if there has been a significant increase in the dropout rate at the local high school and that increase corresponds to the increase of vandalism, the increased dropout rate may, indeed, be the cause of the increase in vandalism. Or if a significant increase in the employment rate of adults in the community correlates with the increase in vandalism, this high employment rate may be the cause of the increase in vandalism. The dropout rate and the employment rate are both plausible causes in this hypothetical example.

As we have discussed throughout this chapter, causal reasoning is complex, and even careful reasoners can go awry in assigning effects to causes and causes to effects. In trying to reason with a partner or an audience about a cause-and-effect relationship, the best you can hope for is to establish a high degree of probability that your claim is correct. Only scientists in the controlled conditions of a laboratory can conclusively demonstrate cause-and-effect relationships. Yet because the carefully controlled conditions of laboratories do not exist outside them, the conclusions scientists draw often do not explain the "human barnyards" beyond the lab. However, the principles just discussed can help you be a more careful causal reasoner about things that can be otherwise.

Causality and the Ends of Reasoning

Like many other troubling incidents in our shared world, both incidents that opened this chapter—The University of Texas tower shootings and the rampage at Wedgwood Baptist Church—raise many, many causal questions. In the first book written about the tower shootings, author Gary Lavergne argued that the cause of the tragedy was that the shooter, Charles J. Whitman, was evil (*Sniper in the Tower,* 1998). Lavergne ruled out several other causal factors—Whitman's upbringing, his use of amphetamines, a small tumor in his brain—and argued instead that "Charles Whitman knew that what he was doing was evil." Similarly, after the shootings in Fort Worth, Texas, Governor George Bush said, "There is a wave of evil passing through America."

Just as it is hard to argue with chance or myth as a causal factor, it is very difficult to argue with such claims about inherent evil. More importantly, while evil might function for some audiences and reasoning partners as an answer to forensic questions, it does little to help provide guidance for deliberative questions raised by such tragedies: What should we do?

Remembering that, as we discussed in Chapter 2, reasoning has three different ends, times, and genres—forensic, epideictic, and deliberative—causal reasoning can be central to finding answers other than just how things happened in the past. Reasoning through language about causes and consequences, complex and tricky as it surely is, remains the best hope we have for figuring out how to keep such tragedies from happening again.

❖ *Reasoning Practice*

1. Read the following news story from the September 11, 1999, *St. Petersburg [Florida] Times*. Then, invent as many causal accounts as you can related to this story.

Park Sued Over Whale Death
Mike Brassfield

Two months ago, a marijuana-smoking drifter named Daniel P. Dukes hid in SeaWorld after it closed. He evaded security guards, stripped to swim trunks and jumped into an icy pool with the park's biggest killer whale.

The 11,000-pound predator played with him like a toy until he drowned.

Now Dukes' parents are suing SeaWorld.

Michael and Patricia Dukes of Columbia, S.C., filed a wrongful-death lawsuit Friday in Orlando alleging that SeaWorld was negligent for not putting better barriers around the whale's tank.

The lawsuit also says SeaWorld misleads the public by giving its killer whales a warm and fuzzy "Shamu" image of "human-loving, funny, sweet, sensitive, touchable, huggable, kissable, approachable, trusting animals."

SeaWorld officials couldn't be reached Friday evening. But they repeatedly have said the park tells audiences the whales are wild animals and predators—they are, after all, called killer whales. They also note that Dukes' own actions led to his death.

Dukes, 27, dived into a tank with the 5-ton mammal sometime before dawn July 6.

2. Find at least four news articles on public debates over the teaching of evolution and creationism in schools. Underline the causal claims in the articles—both those of the writers and those of their sources. Refer to Some Guidelines for Causal Reasoning on pages 90–92, and note whether each causal claim adheres to the guidelines.

3. After the shootings in Littleton, Colorado, in April 1999, many people claimed that playing video games makes children and teenagers more violent, whereas many others claimed that there is no causal connection.

   • Ask at least four people about their views of the causal relation between video games and violence.

   • Then think or write by yourself, reasoning internally about your views of the relationship between playing video games and violent behavior.

   • Finally, think about how you might try to reason with someone who disagrees with you on the causal relationship between video games and violence. How might you find common ground on this topic?

6

Values

Judgments Grounded in Nature and Consequences

I arrive home from work and, with my spouse, open the day's mail. As we go through the several envelopes, Keith remarks, "Wow. I like that bank statement." I wait a few seconds and then wonder out loud: "What do you mean, you like the bank statement? On what grounds do you like the bank statement? How does one *like* a bank statement?"

Aren't you glad you aren't married to a rhetorician?

In any case, some reasoning ensues between us about how Keith could like a bank statement. In this case, he says, he likes the way the bank has redesigned the statement. I wonder out loud whether aesthetic criteria are important in evaluating a bank statement; isn't the correctness of that bottom line what is important about a bank statement? Keith counters that as a graphic designer, he has every right to like the redesign of the bank statement, and he punctuates our reasoning by reminding me that good design is functional as well as aesthetic, thankyouverymuch. We move on to the next piece of mail.

Reasoning about whether something is good or bad, better or worse, functional or dysfunctional, beautiful or repulsive—and all other such claims about the **qualities** of things—is reasoning about **values.**

And reasoning about values is at the heart of what rhetoric can invent and facilitate: When people who hold different values want or need to reason together, rhetoric provides the means for them to do so.

Whereas claims at the stasis of definition have *nouns* as their predicates, claims at the stasis of value most often have *adjectives* as their predicates. A definition of a bank statement might be something like this:

A bank statement is a kind of form.

Note that *kind of form* is a noun phrase. But an evaluation of a bank statement might be something like this:

This bank statement is easy to read.

Note here that the adjective *easy* distinguishes this claim as one about a value—as evaluative. Often, the evaluative phrase in the predicate will be a phrase consisting of an adjective and a noun—for instance:

She was the best mechanic.

He is an incompetent broker.

Occasionally, an evaluative term will be only a noun, but it will carry a value connotation with it:

Elmo is a knave.

Jean turned out to be a savior.

Generally, however, claims at the stasis of value will take this form: *Noun is adjective.*

As I have suggested earlier in this book, reasoning often moves directly to the stases of value and procedure. We make many evaluative claims every day, usually without being aware that we are doing so:

The Astros are incredible!

That movie was stupid.

Your hair looks great.

That t-shirt is tacky.

Youth culture in the United States has for some time now relied on a default evaluative claim: *That sucks.* When we make evaluative statements like these, we usually are expressing our opinions without much reflection, and we do not necessarily expect others to accept our opinions. Similarly, sometimes our evaluative statements represent only our personal tastes:

> This salsa is much better than that one.
>
> I can't stand to listen to Lyle Lovett.
>
> That rose is the most beautiful thing I've ever seen.
>
> I just can't eat fried green tomatoes.

These are expressions of taste, and while they might form the basis for reasoning about questions of value, they often float through the air and hit the ground without consequence.

If we want others to accept our evaluations and to understand the values that underlie them, however, we have to present some arguments that justify or support those evaluations. In this chapter, we will call these justifications and support **criteria.** Criteria are the grounds of value arguments; without them, there is no way for people with different values and differing evaluations to understand each other's points of view or to reason productively. Part of the purpose of this chapter is not only to make you more aware of the value judgments you make but also to enrich your ability to make and support claims of value that allow reasoning to proceed between and among people with different values.

Criteria

The foundation for all arguments that try to persuade others to accept our evaluations is a set of criteria. *Criteria* are standards or norms or grounds on which evaluations are based, explicitly or implicitly. That is, in a way similar to how we deal with stipulative definitions (discussed in Chapter 4), we either leave our criteria implicit or we lay them out for our reasoning partners and audiences to examine. Whether explicit or implicit, our criteria must be there or our evaluations will be groundless. This means that reasoning about values just as often involves reasoning about criteria as it involves reasoning about the value judgments themselves.

Evaluative claims and their grounds provide good reminders of the structure of claim and support—what we called **enthymemes** in Chapter 2. Using the example that opened this chapter, we can see how a claim at the stasis of value that is put together with the criteria that support the claim creates the structure of an enthymeme:

> This bank statement is a good one
>
> because it is easy to read.

The premise that is missing is that *Things that are easy to read are good*. In the case of reasoning about values, that missing premise usually suggests the criteria for evaluation. If your audience or reasoning partner shares your criteria for evaluation, you might be able to keep those criteria implicit. Otherwise, you will not only likely have to make them explicit but also perhaps justify and defend them, as well.

If a reasoner makes the statement *Abortion is immoral,* he or she may need to spend more time laying out and justifying criteria for what is moral and immoral than supporting the main claim about abortion. If the reasoners do not agree what criteria constitute immorality, there is little chance that they will agree on the evaluative judgment about the topic in question.

Here is another example: If you want to convince the citizens of your city that the new statue in front of the courthouse is beautiful, you would likely have to make clear to your audience—your reasoning partners—what your norms for artistic beauty are, either explicitly or implicitly. Those norms might include graceful lines, verisimilitude, proportion, and symmetry—traditional aesthetic norms. However, if the statue were not traditional but avant garde, you might have to lay out another set of aesthetic norms: symbolic rather than mimetic form, errant lines, daring asymmetry, shock value. In either case, if your audience does not share your norms for judging beauty, you will have to argue that the criteria you are using are reasonable for the kind of art the statue represents. The more traditional the statue, the less time and effort you might have to expend in finding a common ground or having the audience identify with your criteria. The more unusual the statue, the more time and effort it might take to gain acceptance of your criteria. Further, some audiences might not accept your account of what comprises the norms for *traditional* or *avant garde* art, and you might have to argue those, as well.

Supporting Value Claims:
Nature and Consequences

There are two basic means of evaluating something—by its nature and by its consequences. As we discussed briefly in Chapter 5, evaluating something by its *consequences* requires a combination of causal and evaluative reasoning. If the consequences of a thing are negative, the thing itself can be said to be bad. If the consequences of a thing are positive, the thing itself can be said to be good. When evaluating something by its consequences, your criteria come from what the thing does or what it causes.

Defining something by its *nature* requires a structure similar to definition, what some rhetoricians call *the ideal X*. Say you want to evaluate a computer by its nature; your criteria come from a list of characteristics of an ideal computer. Then you compare the computer you are evaluating to that constructed ideal. When evaluating something by its nature, your criteria come from what you—and your reasoning partners—agree the thing should be like.

One Example of Claims
about Value: Music

The following music review from the *Austin American-Statesman* (March 9, 1999) offers a good example of the necessity of criteria in arguments about value. As you read Michael Corcoran's review of *Ghosts of Hallelujah* by the Austin band the Gourds, note the implicit as well as the explicit criteria for his positive evaluation and look for whether he is evaluating the music by its nature or by its consequences.

"Ghosts of Hallelujah": The Gourds
Michael Corcoran

Coming out of nowhere is the third full-length disc by Austin's Gourds. And guess what? It's the band's most consistently satisfying album. Recorded in a week, the new record is equal parts "Ghosts" and "Hallelujah," melding the haunting lyricism of "Dem's Good Beeble" (1995) with the wild-eyed jumble of last year's "Stadium Blitzer." As the songs of Jimmy Smith and Kevin Russell resonate deeper, the Gourds are starting to shed their country-roots band skin, even as they've added Max Johnson on fiddle and banjo.

This album may lack a mandolin-fueled hoedown stomper that rivals "Lament" ("Grievin' and Smokin'" comes close), plus fans of Smith's brand of 3 a.m. wharf-rock may be disappointed, but in the end, this is a songwriter's album, where the tunes stand on craft and melody instead of chops and swagger. Rather than going up and down in energy and tone throughout the course of the album, "Ghosts of Hallelujah" holds steady by following one great song with another. Little moods are created not by grouping songs of similar tempo but by the way they seem to connect with each other. Sequencing an album, especially when you've got two distinctly different songwriters, is a little like putting certain animals together in a cage. Here you've got ferrets playing with raccoons and snakes cozied up to opossums like they're all part of the same kingdom.

As evidenced by their showstopping version of Snoop Doggy Dogg's "Gin and Juice," the Gourds' specialty is throwing together the current and the traditional, framing modern experiences next to a musicologist degree. "County Orange," for instance, creates the alt rock zydeco genre to retell Smith's overnight stay at the county jail last year. "Gangsta Lean" puts our boyz in the 'hood, bemoaning the gangster glorification that's snuffed too many futures. "Gangsta lean, gangsta lean, you done killed 'em all," Russell sings in his mournful mountain tenor. "You can't tell me it doesn't bother you."

"Rugged Roses" shouldn't go unmentioned. A wedding present to Russell and his wife Robin, the song is Smith at his most attractively vulnerable best. It's a magical melody, but he seems to regard it like a lint-covered dime, as though he could pull it out anytime with ease. Everything that's great about the Gourds can also be heard on "January 6," a sweet Russell song with teeth. It sounds almost like a KASE hit, so engaging is the melody and so snappy are the drums. But this song doesn't know how to line dance. It doesn't drink Coors Light. There's no sponsorship, no manipulation. The song doesn't even really have a name: "January 6" was the day Russell wrote it.

The Gourds are the great unfinished band. These unfocused screw-ups will never be huge, not like their sister band the Damnations. But the Gourds' progression is a thing to behold: They remain creatively vital and we keep listening because there's nothing more exciting for a fan than to chart a favorite band's growth, then to be on hand to hear them plop into their talent without a trace of doubt.

What criteria did you uncover? While Corcoran keeps most of his criteria implicit, it is clear that he values the disc for its consistent quality, its emphasis on songwriting, its combination of current and traditional styles, and its importance as a chronicle of a talented band's progression and growth. Corcoran values the CD for how closely it conforms to his sense of the ideal X.

How Corcoran supports the few criteria he makes explicit also suggests what understanding he has of his audience: His comment that "This song doesn't know how to line dance. It doesn't drink Coors Light" suggests that neither do readers who are prone to share his evaluation of the Gourds. It is also fairly obvious that Corcoran's audience is Austinites who—whether they get out to the music venues or not—generally like to fancy themselves connected to the live music scene. Further, his review appeared in the weekly entertainment section of the newspaper, which would likely be foreign to those not already interested in the local music scene.

Finally, the criterion with which Corcoran chooses to end the review is perhaps the most telling about what underlies his positive review of *Ghosts of Hallelujah:* The Gourds are good because they will never make it big. The best bands, Corcoran's implicit criterion seems to suggest, are never the ones that become hugely popular but that folks are still willing to follow for years.

Another Example: Family Farms

Whereas the music review example might help you think about how to make value arguments in conversation, in class, or for the local radio station or newspaper, the following example of reasoning about values suggests just how complicated value arguments can be when values about public issues are in conflict. The following interview from National Public Radio's *Weekend All Things Considered* (May 29, 1999) presents a clash of values as represented in attitudes toward agriculture across the twentieth century in the United States—a topos that affects each of us, whether we are aware of it or not.

As you read, again be careful to notice the criteria that underlie the value claims of the various speakers and whether the evaluations are based on the nature of a thing, on its consequences, or on both. Reasoning about value can be most difficult when the nature and consequences of a thing are at odds.

Daniel Zwerdling, Host: People of every religion are trying to figure out how to marry ancient traditions to modern life. And one group of Americans are trying to figure out how to prevent its traditions from disappearing. We're talking about family farmers. A hundred years ago, nearly half the population lived on the land. Today it's less than 2 percent, but they're producing more food than ever. Here on NPR we've been exploring how technology has redefined our lives during this past century, and NPR's Dan Charles continues the series by considering how farmers adopted mass production and helped make themselves an endangered species.

Dan Charles, Reporter: The easiest work Tom Cunningham ever did on the farm, he said, was plow a single furrow walking behind a mule.

Tom Cunningham: I could take a mule and walk all day long, just one mule, and I'm kind of guessing now because my memory's not good enough to know, but maybe I would plow one acre of cotton. I could do it all day and ride a bicycle all night. I mean, it wouldn't— it just didn't tire me out.

Charles: Cunningham grew cotton near Darlington, South Carolina, starting early in the century. His memories are part of an oral history of Southern farming collected by the Smithsonian Institution. But by that time, a new type of agriculture already was taking shape out in California. Steven Stoll, a historian at Yale University, says it was the product of a revolutionary mentality, a Gold Rush attitude toward the land.

Steven Stoll, Historian, Yale University: California agriculture was established by a group of people who were unlike other kinds of American farmers. They were capitalists. And the context in which they came to California was the Gold Rush. They came wanting to make money.

Charles: They thought and acted on a grand scale.

Stoll: They bought up gigantic pieces of land. They planted farms 10,000, 20,000, even 30,000 acres—farms the size of entire counties.

Charles: These capitalist farmers built locomotives for the land, steam-powered tractors that pulled enormous plows. They saw the world as their market. They sent wheat off to England in enormous cargo ships and oranges or tomatoes to Chicago and New York in refrigerated rail cars.

Stoll: The most perishable kinds of commodities would be sold in the most distant cities for consumption by people who generally had no idea where they came from or how they were grown.

Charles: The idea behind California agriculture, harnessing science and industrial technology to the job of farming, became the definition of something called *progressive agriculture.* The U.S. Department of Agriculture, with its network of scientists and local extension agents, promoted it all across the country, and farmers took to it. Starting in the 1920s they bought tractors in great numbers, replacing the horses that used to pull plows and planters and threshing machines. They planted more productive hybrid corn, purchased from commercial seed companies, and they brought in combined reaping-threshing machines, so-called combines, to handle the harvest. John Laney of Lyon, Mississippi, also interviewed for the Smithsonian's history project, said many farmers had a sentimental attachment to the old ways of doing things, plowing with animals, for instance, instead of noisy, smoke-belching gasoline tractors.

John Laney: Some people would shake their heads and say, "Oh, no, I'll never have one on my place." But boy, just as soon as he saw what his neighbor was going to do—as they got able, they started getting them.

Charles: Tractors were more powerful than horses, and you didn't have to feed them a quarter of your grain harvest. Having one was also a status symbol. It showed you were forward-looking, progressive. Although another Southern farmer, John Dillard, recalls that his wife, Neoma, wasn't too impressed.

John Dillard: Her and this lady was hoeing and every time I'd pass them I'd holler, "Look, honey, I'm riding." Well, I kept on till I made her mad, and she come up behind the tractor and got on the cultivator and I didn't know she was even on the cultivator till she hit me with that switch.

Neoma Dillard: I come right down his back with it, kerplunk.

John Dillard: She didn't have no mercy.

Neoma Dillard: Well, you didn't have none on me.

Pete Daniel, Historian, National Museum of American History: Most Americans, when faced with a machine, will accept it. I mean, that's part of our heritage; we don't stand around and say, "Well, I wonder if this machine is going to really help us."

Charles: In the long run, according to agricultural economists, new technology on the farm didn't make farmers more prosperous. The people who really benefited were urban consumers who got cheaper food. Steven Stoll from Yale University says the reason is something called the *agricultural treadmill.*

Stoll: If you understand only one thing about agricultural economics, just one thing, it is that farmers do not set their own prices. They take a price; they do not set a price.

Charles: When farmers produce more food, they saturate the market. People can eat only so much. Prices fall, so farmers have to produce more and more efficiently just to earn the same amount. During the early 1930s, farmers on the southern Great Plains tried to keep up by working the land harder and harder. It helped create the Dust Bowl.

Charles: Franklin Roosevelt's first Secretary of Agriculture, Henry Wallace, tried to get the treadmill under control. As part of the New Deal, he put in place programs to pay farmers to pull land out of production.

Unidentified Man (from Smithsonian audiotape): When farmers turn out more than the market will take, it would be foolish to call upon insects and diseases and soil erosion and depletion of fertility to cut down the volume. The wise policy, just as in industry, is to produce efficiently the volume the markets need.

Charles: Wallace wanted both things, limits on production but also more efficient production with new technology. Once again, progressive agriculture. Pete Daniel from the National Museum of American History says government officials had a kind of blueprint of the ideal American farm in their minds. It had plenty of land and the latest equipment but not many people. The South, though, was a whole different world.

Daniel: What you have are these small farms, poor housing, hardly any machinery, and a lot of sharecroppers and tenants who didn't own land. They did not fit the blueprint.

Charles: That blueprint for agriculture and New Deal programs for cutting production were a disaster for those tenant farmers and sharecroppers. Large landowners, most of them white, decided what land to take out of production. They weren't supposed to, but they often pocketed the federal payments and told sharecroppers who'd worked that land to leave. Then, after World War II, a whole new set of technologies arrived.

Daniel: The cotton harvester, within 15 years, was harvesting 80 percent of the cotton. You had herbicides, which were doing what the hoe people had done with their hoes, chopping cotton. So you got rid of all that labor. You didn't need people anymore.

Charles: Pete Daniel says this fact had a profound effect on the struggle for civil rights in the South. When white landowners were faced with the threat of integration, they fought it, but they also had another less openly confrontational option: They could buy more machinery and force black farm workers out of the county or out of the state. Industrial jobs were beckoning in Northern cities. Millions of African American families migrated from the countryside to cities and from South to North.

Daniel: I believe that, had there not been mechanization and a falling-off in labor demand, that there would have been a great deal more violence, because black people were challenging the power of the white power structure.

Charles: It's corn planting time in southern Maryland, and Mike Dunn is driving his aging Farmall tractor hard. He sprayed this field a few days ago to kill the weeds; now the planting drill drives rows of corn seed, pretreated with insecticide, into the hard, unplowed soil. Dunn can plant about 50 acres a day, all by himself. He has to; he has 500 acres to plant. That's not much these days, he says; just a hobby farm, really.

Mike Dunn, Farmer: To be able to support, say, a $30,000-a-year income, you'd probably have to have well over 500 acres for one person, and that's probably a pretty dirt-poor living.

Charles: Even big farmers with 1,000 or 2,000 acres aren't doing very well these days. Corn and soybean prices are down again. When Mike Dunn harvests his soybean crop this fall, he'll probably get less for it per bushel than farmers have in 30 years. And every time the U.S. Department of Agriculture releases a new batch of statistics, the trend is the same: fewer farms, larger farms, and fewer farmers. That trend has provoked much soul searching. Many Americans have long held a romantic image of farm life. Thomas Jefferson and many after him believed that independent, self-reliant farmers were the foundation of American democracy.

But the romantic image of life on the farm hasn't been reality for a long time for most farmers. It's a large-scale, profit-maximizing business, increasingly dominated by technology.

What value claims did you notice as you read this transcript? Early on, one farmer claimed that plowing with a mule was easy. Do you recall his criterion for that evaluation? He said he didn't feel tired at the end of the day, even though such plowing was hard physical work.

What other claims at the stasis of value did you notice? Someone else claimed that tractors were more powerful than horses and that they were superior because farmers didn't need to feed them significant portions of their grain harvest. Notice how that combines (no pun intended) evaluation by nature (the criterion of power) with evaluation by consequences (no loss of grain harvest).

Notice also how causal reasoning—sometimes chains of causes and consequences—provide criteria for value judgments: The cotton harvester made cotton farming more efficient but it also put people out of work, contributing, in large part, to the great migration of African American workers from the rural South to the North and Midwest in the 1930s and 1940s. And agricultural machinery in general enabled farmers to produce more food, which is arguably good; yet that increase in production led to a saturation of the market and the consequent lowering of prices and bankruptcy of many family farmers.

Did you notice the two evaluations by *the ideal X* in the transcript above? One is *the blueprint,* as it was called above, for farms under *Progressive Agriculture.* Southern farms did not fit that blueprint—or ideal X—and thus suffered consequences. Another is the *Jeffersonian ideal—* or *romantic ideal,* as the reporter calls it—of the family farm as central to democracy. How do current farms compare to that ideal?

Most striking in this example of a discourse that offers various evaluations of agricultural technology is the contrast between the nature of the thing and its consequences. The consequences of technology have been generally negative for family farms—making them endangered species—even though the consequences for suburban and urban consumers have been generally positive: more abundant produce and other farm products at lower prices. One of the sources in the transcript suggests that thinking about the consequences—*Will this machine really help us?*—of technology might be superior (notice the value judgment!) to just assuming technology is good by its nature.

Weighting Criteria

Particularly when there is a clash of values—as, in the previous example, the positive consequences of agricultural technology for suburbanites and city dwellers juxtaposed with the negative consequences for family farmers—reasoners have to rank, or *weight,* their criteria for evaluation before they can make a value judgment. As the ancient sophists first pointed out, the same wind can feel warm to some people and cool to others. That the same phenomenon is judged differently by different people, different communities, and different cultures should be no surprise. But when reasoners are called upon to make judgments, sometimes ranking or weighting the criteria for evaluation can help reasoning proceed.

Similar to the process of justifying or defending criteria that we discussed earlier in this chapter, you may need to defend or justify how you weight particular criteria when you make and support claims at the stasis of value. In Corcoran's review of the Gourds, for instance, he explicitly ranks the criterion of a band's progress very highly. He implicitly ranks musical and genre experimentation highly, as well. Much lower in his list of criteria would come polished sound, consistency of performance, and other similar criteria that many music fans would rank as much more important. Like formulating criteria themselves, weighting criteria is an important part of supporting reasoning at the stasis of value. As always, your reasoning partners or audiences will help you invent not only the criteria for your evaluation but also how you might rank or weight those criteria.

Guidelines for Reasoning about Values

Keep in mind these guidelines as you reason about values:

- *Decide what evaluative claim you want to make about the subject you will be discussing.* Let's say, for example, that you are reasoning with someone about leasing, rather than buying, a new car. You want to argue that, in some cases, leasing a new car is less expensive than buying a new car.

- *Express that claim for yourself in a single sentence, using adjectives (X is fancy), nouns (X is a traitor), or adjective and noun phrases (X is the perfect boss).* Here are some other examples of value claims:
  Volunteer work is beneficial for the whole community.
  Democracy is the best form of government.
  The mayor's project proved to be a disaster.

- *Determine the criterion or criteria upon which you will evaluate the subject you are reasoning about.* For example, one criterion upon which you might base an argument that leasing a car is cheaper than buying it is that the prospective lessor does not have to make a down payment, which is normally needed to buy a car.

- *Make clear to your audience your criteria for making the evaluative judgment.* If the criteria upon which you are basing your argument are not self-evident or obvious—or particularly if they are arguable—you should reveal your criteria explicitly.

- *Consider explaining or justifying your criteria, based on who your reasoning partner or audience is.* An explanation or justification may be necessary if the audience does not readily see the relevance or applicability of your criteria to the subject of your evaluative reasoning.

- *Also consider weighting your criteria.* Doing so is particularly valuable if you are using more than one criterion or if whatever you are evaluating is surrounded, like the example of agricultural technology, by clashes of values or by conflicting evaluations by nature and by consequences.

- *Show that the particular thing you are evaluating does or does not meet your criteria.* Meeting this obligation is crucial for the success of your argument. Even though your audience may agree on the criteria for evaluation, they must also agree that the particular thing you are evaluating meets those criteria.

- *Remember that comparative and superlative evaluations take extra work.* Comparing two things and claiming one is better than the other requires (in addition to the points already mentioned) that you apply your evaluative criteria to both things you are comparing—or all things, if you are comparing more than two. In other words, arguing that something is *better* or *the best* requires more comprehensive application of criteria than just claiming something is *good*.

Again, we make evaluations all the time—at work, at home, and on the way back and forth. Frequently, we express those evaluations for others to hear or to read, and sometimes, we are called upon to justify our evaluations. When we have to defend our evaluations, we need to make our criteria explicit in order to begin to persuade others of the reasonableness of our judgments—or even to find some common ground for others to understand our values and judgments. Sometimes, we have to spend as much time explaining and justifying our criteria as we do defending our judgments. If we cannot justify our criteria and the weight or emphasis we have given them to the satisfaction of our reasoning partners—spouses, co-workers, fellow citizens, or even ourselves—we will not likely be very secure in the values of our own judgments.

❖ *Reasoning Practice*

1. Read the following account of friendship, taught by Aristotle in "Nichomachean Ethics" during the fourth century before the common era. As you reread, mark the claims of value. And as you read the text a third time, note the criteria on which the value claims are made.

Only the friendship of those who are good, and similar in their goodness, is perfect. For these people each alike wish good for the other *qua* good, and they are good in themselves. And it is those who desire the good of their friends for the friends' sake that are most truly friends, because each loves the other for what he is, and not for any incidental quality. Accordingly the friendship of such men lasts so long as they remain good; and goodness is an enduring quality. Also each party is good both absolutely and for his friend, since the good are both good absolutely and to each other; because everyone is pleased with his own conduct and conduct that resembles it, and the conduct of good men is the same or similar. Friendship of this kind is permanent, reasonably enough; because in it are united all the attributes that friends ought to possess. For all friendship has as its object something good or pleasant—either absolutely or relatively to the person who feels the affection—and is based on some similarity between the parties. But in this friendship all the qualities that we have mentioned belong to the friends themselves; because in it there is similarity, etc.; and what is absolutely good is also absolutely pleasant; and these are the most lovable qualities. Therefore it is between good men that both love and friendship are chiefly found and in the highest form.

That such friendships are rare is natural, because men of this kind are few. And in addition they need time and intimacy; for as the saying goes, you cannot get to know each other until you have eaten the proverbial quantity of salt together. Nor can one man accept another, or the two become friends, until each has proved to the other that he is worthy of love, and so won his trust. Those who are quick to make friendly advances to each other have the desire to be friends, but they are not unless they are worthy of love and know it. The wish for friendship develops rapidly, but friendship does not.

This kind of friendship, then, is perfect both in point of duration and in all other respects; and in it each party receives from the other benefits that are in all respects the same or similar, as ought to be the case between friends.

2. Make a list of your criteria for what constitutes a friend. Get in pairs, as your teacher suggests, or discuss with a friend what his or her criteria for friendship are. What criteria do you and the other person agree on? Which do you disagree on? What consequences does your disagreement have for your actions?

3. Evaluate Aristotle's account of friendship, and support it with criteria. Use your own experiences as well as anecdotes from others and public accounts of friendship to support your claims.

4. Find a recent evaluation of your school, college, university, city, or state. What value judgment is being made? On what criteria is it based? Are the criteria explicit or implicit? What accounts for the fact that the ranking likely changes every year? What is your evaluation of the evaluation? What are your criteria for your evaluation?

7

Procedures and Proposals

Actualizing the Potential for Change

Ready?

Do you want to change the world? This chapter offers you some ways to begin. **Procedure arguments** allow reasoners to try, through discourse, to change the state of things in our shared worlds.

Whereas conjecture, definition, cause, and value concern primarily forensic and epideictic questions—initiated by a need for judgment about the past or the present—the stasis of procedure is fundamentally concerned with the future. Of course many different kinds of discourses can serve **deliberative** purposes: Popular songs and films, for instance, can be future oriented in significant ways. But claims and arguments at the stasis of procedure—*Let's throw the tea into the harbor!*—are fundamentally geared to *change* and pointed toward *the future*.

Procedure arguments, or *proposals,* concern advocating what a reasoner or group of reasoners has concluded is the best way to effect some change. A reasoner arguing at the stasis of procedure tries to convince his or her reasoning partners or audiences that what he or she proposes or recommends is *the best way to achieve an objective.* The objective may be, for instance, to improve a product and at the same time lower its cost; to refine a procedure to make it more efficient; to create a more equitable taxation policy; or to change procedures or standards to ensure that an outcome is more representative, more inclusive, or more just. Specifically, the objective may be to produce a better wheelchair or a better rainwater-collection system. The objective may be to improve the means of deliberation in a civic group, church, synagogue, or other organization. The objective may be to have the campus food service offer beef burgers along with veggie burgers. The objective may be to plant a tree in memory of a loved one who died in military service. The objective may be to outlaw sentences that start by repeating the same five words.

Regardless of the specific goal, reasoning at the stasis of procedure involves, potentially, all the various kinds of reasoning we have discussed thus far in this book. Reasoners may use **conjectural** arguments to persuade others that *Something is amiss* or *We have a problem here*. Obviously, claims at the stasis of **value** would also help reasoners argue by nature as well as by consequences that X is unjust or dysfunctional. Reasoners need to share **definitions** if they are to understand precisely what the current way of doing things is and how the proposal would change those ways. Reasoning about **causes and consequences** is nearly always involved in claims and arguments about procedures because reasoners have to be able to persuade others that the proposal would actually change things—would actually solve the problem that is understood to exist.

Even so, procedure arguments also entail some unique considerations and strategies. This chapter will introduce you to those considerations and strategies, show you some examples of proposal arguments, and offer you some guidelines and questions to consider as you begin to imagine yourself as a changer of procedures and an inventor of proposals.

"Houston: We Have a Problem"

This infamous line provides a reminder of the first step on the path to reasoning about procedures. Only if you can get others to understand and accept that a problem exists are you likely to move them to any kind of change or action.

As I said earlier, you will likely use claims at the stases of conjecture and value to reason about whether a problem exists; you will use causal claims to argue that the problem is the consequence of some situation or other procedure. If your audience or reasoning partners already agree that a problem exists, you might be able to jump right in with a proposal. More often, however, you will need to spend time reasoning together at the stases of conjecture and value before you can dig in at the stasis of procedure.

As we discussed briefly in Chapter 1, Aristotle's understanding of how change occurs in living things offers us a way to think about how change can occur through discourse. In his treatise *On the Soul*, Aristotle distinguished between **potential** (*dunamis*) and **actualized potential** (*energia*). One way to think of reasoning at the stasis of procedure is that it actualizes a potential for change that already exists in your reasoning partners, readers, or listeners. In other words, you might want to imagine your reasoning as having the potential to energize yourself, another person, or a group to change their ways. Rhetoric itself, according to Aristotle, was a faculty or power or potential for finding all the available means of persuasion. The reasoner, through his or her discourses, holds the power to change himself or herself through internal reasoning and to change other people and their practices through external reasoning.

That reasoning about procedures can actualize others only after there is agreement or identification about whether a problem exists suggests a structural image for invention at the stasis of procedure: the hourglass.

Visualize an hourglass in your mind. Think of the top half as providing a place for you to think about inventions concerning whether a problem exists: What's the problem? Why is it a problem? What are its causes? What are its consequences—and for whom? What makes it a problem for your audience? Who is your audience? Is your audience already aware of the problem? In what ways is your problem also their problem? What can your audience realistically do about this problem? Why is this audience worth persuading?

The bottom half of the hourglass provides a place for inventions about how the proposal will solve the problems and what other advantages it may have: What is your proposal? Why and how would it solve the problem? What are the advantages of your proposal? Is it feasible?

How do you know? Is it plausible? Why hasn't anyone suggested it or tried it before? Why is it better than other proposals that have tried to solve the same problem?

The base of the hourglass provides a place for thinking about what objections others might have to the proposal—and there are always lots of reasons offered for not changing things! Human beings at rest—like energy itself, as described in the second law of thermodynamics—tend to remain at rest. That is to say, there often seem to be many more reasons *not* to change things than to change them—another reason why arguments at the stasis of procedure are so difficult to make. With practice, however, you can become more comfortable with the idea of being an agent of change by using the elements of reasoning.

Think about these questions when you imagine the base of the hourglass: What objections to your proposal might your audience raise? What reasons might they have not to do what you propose? Are the objections valid? Are there alternative solutions? How is your proposal preferable to the other possible solutions?

Finally, the top of the hourglass—though the top and base are, of course, interchangeable—is your ethos. What ethos do you have on this topic? Why should your audience listen to you? Why should they change the way they do things because of your arguments? I will have a bit more to say about ethos in discussing credibility later in this chapter (see page 118). As with any argument, the character and credibility of the reasoner is central, but because procedure arguments require people to change or to part with something, the credibility of the speaker is particularly crucial.

With practice, the image of the hourglass—with sands moving through it—can remind you of the potential for movement and change that lies dormant and waiting in procedure and proposal arguments. Will *you* be the actualizer?

A Modest Proposal

Here is a proposal argument written by Courtney Robertson, who was one of my students a few years ago. After she wrote it for class, she submitted it to the city's daily newspaper and received many letters and e-mails in response.

A Hint for UT Students
Courtney Robertson

Recently, Larry Faulkner, the new president of the University of Texas at Austin, stated that he would like to find a way to move students through the university more quickly and more efficiently. As a student, I would like to suggest a way to do just that—make class attendance mandatory.

This week marks the end of my first year at UT. Looking back, I am amazed at how much I have learned about myself and the world around me through wondering, questioning, reading, making mistakes, and, most of all, through attending class. It disturbs me to think of how many students cannot say the same.

Each day that I sit in my math class, I am reminded of how common absences are at UT. When homework is due, I watch student after student enter the auditorium, drop off his or her homework, and leave. When homework is not due, most students do not even bother to show up and one-fourth of the class sits scattered throughout the auditorium. There are times when all 150 of us are present. What is the occasion? Once a month, my math class takes an exam.

I wish I could say this is an unusual class at UT–Austin. I wish I could say that my other courses are attended by students on regular days and exam days alike. But I cannot; the only classes that have good attendance that I have been to are the ones where students are penalized if they do not show up.

Some may say that class attendance is a choice; after all, we are not in high school anymore. I agree. In fact, if the only people who were affected by poor class attendance were those who skip class, I would not consider this to be such a large problem. But this is not the case.

Last week, a student who does not regularly attend class walked up to our math professor, showed her one of the problems that he missed on an exam, and challenged her ability to teach because he could not answer the question correctly. Both he and our professor became angry, but one left the classroom, and the other stayed to lecture. The week before, I found it hard to review my notes before a classics exam because of two girls who were loudly complaining about everything from what the professor wore to how the material was not relevant to their lives. Eventually, one whispered, "Well, we haven't been to class in a month," and they burst into laughter.

Whatever prevents a student from coming to class, required attendance will help alleviate the problems these students create. For the student who avoids a true evaluation of herself by missing class, she will either discover her abilities through attending class or she will continue to avoid evaluation outside of the university.

For the student who misses class because he is unsure whether he belongs in college, he will be more able to appraise his situation if he attends his classes. For the student whose sole excuse for not attending class is laziness, she will have a very important decision to make—either go to class or risk failing out. For the student who refuses to attend class because he believes that he learns nothing from it, he will learn otherwise. Finally, the student who already attends class regularly will enjoy the greatest benefit of a required attendance policy—an increase in the academic reputation of UT.

The best way for Dr. Faulkner to begin his presidency of UT is to re-emphasize what the university is here for and what the university's top priority is—academics. If one listens to the conversations of students, one will discover that among the most frequently asked questions is "Are you going to class today?" Let UT answer that question for its students; we have enough students as it is, so come to UT to attend class or do not come to UT at all.

There should be no in between—there should be no college without class.

Feasibility, Plausibility, Credibility

I probably do not have to tell you that Courtney's proposal has not yet been implemented. As you continue to read this chapter, think about why that might be so.

One of the strategies unique to procedure arguments is **feasibility**. You and your reasoning partners might propose something that all agree should be done or made—for instance, that all first-year students should live on campus or that commercial television networks should let presidential candidates advertise for free. But if your procedure or proposal cannot be accomplished—or cannot be accomplished easily or inexpensively—it probably will not win acceptance, unless you propose a means to fund it and carry it out. You cannot just assert that what you are proposing *can* be done; you must show *how* it can be done and convince your audience that it can best be done in that way.

A group of students who wanted to reopen the observation deck of The University of Texas tower and another who wanted a statue of the Reverend Dr. Martin Luther King, Jr., placed on the UT campus were told for years that their proposals were not feasible. The students continued to revise their proposals, however, and over time, both proposals resulted in change. The observation deck is open again, and the statue of King, only the second on a college campus in the United States, stands on the university's east mall. So remember that feasibility, like many other issues we have discussed, is arguable. Rarely should it be understood as the final word on a proposal.

Another consideration you will have to address when you are reasoning and advocating at the stasis of procedure is the **plausibility** of the proposal—that is, the *likelihood of the proposal coming to pass.* You might very well be able to establish the feasibility of your procedure or proposal—that it is do-able. But if you cannot establish that your idea will likely succeed, you probably will not be able to get others to go along with it. Implementing a proposal usually entails expenditure of someone's time, effort, or money, and if the proposal seems too risky, you will not likely actualize many others' potential for movement and change.

Another of my students, Nakeenya Haynes, made a compelling argument that the campus community needs a grocery store. She provided a splendid evaluation of the current situation:

> There is no place close to campus to buy fresh produce or other products, and getting to anything other than convenience stores (which have high overhead and small selections) requires lugging grocery bags on buses and risking having what is bought spoil on the trip home.

Many in and outside of class agreed. Yet no matter how positively disposed they were to her idea in theory, all of Nakeenya's readers and listeners doubted that the various institutions and businesses that needed to work together to get a grocery on campus would do so. Why should Nakeenya's problem be *their* problem? No matter how good her idea, until she can argue that it is plausible, it is unlikely to happen. Still, she continues to work on it undaunted. (Right, Nakeenya?) She believes that a local grocery store is essential to a community, and perhaps someday she and others will be able to actualize her great idea.

Finally, as with all other kinds of reasoning, the chance for success of a procedure or proposal argument depends on the **credibility** of the reasoner or advocate. We have discussed *ethos* briefly twice before, and we need to reiterate it here as it applies to proposals. In order to have others go along with your ideas for changing procedures and adopting proposals, they must trust your capabilities and your judgments. *Through your reasoning,* you need to establish yourself as a reliable authority on the matter under discussion. Otherwise, you will not be able to actualize others to follow you in bringing your proposal to fruition.

Guidelines for Reasoning about Procedures and Proposals

Follow these guidelines when reasoning about procedures and proposals:

- *Designate the problem.* Projects that involve arguing about the best way to make or do something—to effect some change—are usually prompted by a problem of some sort. As the image of the hourglass as an inventional structure will remind you, your first task is to reason about what the problem is and then bring others to identify with you about it. You must be able to persuade those who have the power to change the procedure or to bring your proposal to fruition that the current situation is a problem for them, too. The hourglass can also remind you of the Greek sense of time called *kairos,* which we discussed in Chapters 1 and 2. Kairos is an important part of any argument, but it is central to reasoning with others about change.

- *Define the problem.* Once you have pointed out the problem, give your reasoning partners detailed information about it—describe it, offer some history of it, indicate its causes and its consequences. Do your best to convince the potential adopters of your proposal that there truly is a problem—if they are not already convinced. In either case, make sure through your definitions and other means that all parties agree not only that a problem exists but what the problem is.

- *Develop the consequences.* After you have helped the audience become aware that a problem exists and have made sure that all parties agree on what the problem is, you will need to spend considerable time and reasoning effort to spell out the consequences for various parties of ignoring, rather than solving, the problem. If you can get others to identify with your claims that the consequences of doing nothing will be negative—if not downright disastrous—they will be infinitely more eager to listen to a proposal for change.

As you likely have gathered from reading this chapter, the stasis of procedure is a powerful place from which to generate change, either through internal reasoning in your own life or through external reasoning in the lives and procedures of others. As I said in Chapter 1, practicing rhetoric—reasoning through language—helps you become a better reasoner. Likewise, practicing arguments at the stasis of procedure can help you see yourself as a more active and powerful person. As many of my students have said after submitting their proposal arguments to the local or campus newspaper or to a university staff member or official, reasoning about procedures and proposals can help you see yourself in a different, less passive way. We will talk more about how the practice of rhetoric can change you in Chapter 8. For now, reason some more at the stasis of procedure with the activities that follow.

❖ *Reasoning Practice*

1. Reread Courtney Robertson's proposal argument on pages 115–116. Reason with at least one more person about these questions (which can be used to evaluate any proposal argument):

   - What is the proposal?

   - What problem does the proposal intend to solve?

   - Who is the audience for the proposal? And has the writer done enough to help the audience understand that a problem exists? That is, is the writer's problem also a problem for the audience?

- Would the proposal solve the problem? Would the proposal have any additional advantages?
- What objections will likely be made to the proposal? Are there other, perhaps better possible solutions?
- Does the proposer have ethos, as manifested in her reasoning?
- How is kairos important to the proposal?

2. Is attendance a problem on your campus or in your workplace or organization? If so, what might you propose to solve the problem?

8

Becoming a Citizen Critic

Where Rhetoric Meets the Road

Get to Work
Elizabeth Mims

I have been going to the Ramsey swimming pool since I was 2 years old or at least big enough to wear a bathing suit. Now I am 10 and I still am going to Ramsey pool. But this past summer, we walked from our house to the pool in the sweltering Texas heat, only to find that the pool was closed because the pump needed repairs. The water was too cloudy to see the bottom of the pool. So with sweat pouring down our faces, we waited for the water to be clear enough to swim. Many times we had to turn around and walk back to our house.

We are hoping you have started repairing the pump, so that it will be ready by this summer. We don't want to have the same thing that happened last summer happen this summer.

This letter, published in the *Austin American-Statesman* in February 1999, is an example of citizen criticism. The writer of the letter, Elizabeth

Mims, is a citizen critic. I do not know Elizabeth, but her letter suggests that anyone—even a 10-year-old child—can faithfully affect her world for the better if she has some hope that her public discourse can make a difference.

This chapter will offer you some ideas about how to become a citizen critic. First, I will say a bit more about what I mean by *citizen critic.* Then, we will discuss how identifying common diversions of reasoning offers you a means of critiquing others' reasoning without criticizing them personally. Finally, we will talk about why citizen critics are essential to democracies. The chapter will leave you with ways to think about using reasoning to become a more active citizen of your state or nation, county or township, community or neighborhood, school or workplace. Becoming a citizen critic is a matter of habit; like reasoning itself, it is a matter of habitual practice. Elizabeth Mims manifested her faith in reasoning, writing, and public discourse at an early age, probably at the suggestion and with the aid of an adult. It is my hope that our collective polity and institutions neither extinguish her faith nor fail her.

Not all letters to the editor, I would argue, are written by citizen critics. Citizen criticism requires some sense of faith in whatever public or community is being addressed. Here is another letter to the editor, this one from the *Daily Texan,* the daily student newspaper at The University of Texas at Austin, in which the space for letters to the editor is troped as the "Firing Line." As you read it, compare it to the letter by Elizabeth Mims.

Just Another Club
Adam Demand, RTF Freshman

I can't believe the arrogance of Pam Bowman, Daniela Dwyer, and Stephen Stetson. I'm used to the University throwing away money, but I can't believe these snobs actually believe they deserve their special treatment. You can't possibly be stupid enough to think that your organization [the UT Forensics Team] is anything but another club.

How generous of the Forensics Team to allow fellow students to do their work for them. It's also nice that you allow students to join your club, unlike the infinite number of other clubs on campus that forbid student entry. As for your intercollegiate debates, I have been to one. It was a nice mixture of boring and crap.

I'm sick of self-important organizations like yours that think the University depends solely on them to attract students. I have news for you: Some of us are here to learn and it doesn't really matter what kind of organizations are available. Some of us could also use the 20 cents we have to shell out for an organization that only 70 people actually participate in.

Maybe those 70 people should start footing the bill for their little club. I hope the University cuts your funding and the Forensics Team becomes yet another bad memory for the University of Texas. If I want to listen to insincere, hypocritical nonsense, I'll talk to the faculty.

While there are many differences between Elizabeth's and Adam's letters, the most remarkable one is the hope that Elizabeth shows in her letter and the lack of hope—*hostility* is the word one of my students used when we discussed the letter in class—that Adam shows in his. I do not know Adam, either, but I do wonder why he is at the university. Although it may well be the case that the Forensics Team should not be funded by student fees, why does Adam need to criticize the team members themselves (describing them as arrogant, stupid snobs) and take the entire faculty along with him? If all he gets from the faculty is "insincere, hypocritical nonsense," why would he want to study at the university? It certainly can not be "to learn"; he shows no faith in his professors or his peers. And while it may well be that someone should launch a public discussion about the quality of undergraduate education at this particular university or at universities in general, Adam's letter certainly offers no shareable criteria for doing so—say, evaluating the faculty, class sizes, or the curricula.

Adam's letter is an example of the kind of public discourse that aims to leave nothing standing but the sarcasm of the writer. Even if people respond to the letter, it is unlikely that any productive reasoning about the issues will ensue. Why? The personal attacks Adam makes do not inspire confidence that he would be responsive to any arguments, regardless of their origin or content. Even though it might be persuasive to some readers, Adam's letter does nothing to invite reasoned responses, to encourage publics to form, or to lead to collective judgment about an issue of common concern. How is the public discussion of student fees continued or improved by Adam's reasoning? His letter is to reasoning what road rage is to driving.

Diversions of Reasoning

Rhetoric has for centuries offered a rich lexicon for describing language use in practice. In such a brief chapter, we cannot address that entire lexicon. (Richard Lanham's *Handlist of Rhetorical Terms* [1991] offers a fairly comprehensive list.) However, we do have time to discuss some common diversions of reasoning. The terms and concepts discussed in the rest of this section offer you means of examining and critiquing the reasoning of others without attacking them personally. After all, how can you assume to know what is inside the head or heart of another person—particularly when all you have to go on are their words uttered across a room, on the phone or radio, or in a text you hold in your hands or view via computer?

Overgeneralizing

One very common diversion of reasoning is generalizing without looking at enough cases to support a sweeping conclusion. Everyone does this. (Just kidding: Hear the overgeneralization?) Well, lots of us do. Overgeneralizing happens very often in conversation, but it is common in writing and formal speaking, as well.

We overgeneralize when we draw a conclusion about all the members of a class of things or persons or cars or computers or podiatrists (or anything else) on the basis of a very limited sample. For instance, if someone who has seen only *Forrest Gump* and *Big* declares that *All Tom Hanks movies are stupid,* she is overgeneralizing. One way to avoid overgeneralizing is to qualify your claims; rather than saying all *X*s are *Y* when you have not seen all or even most *X*s, qualify the claim:

> The Tom Hanks movies I've seen have been stupid, but I've only seen two.

Begging the Question

Begging the question occurs when a reasoner makes a statement that assumes the very thing he wants to persuade a reasoning partner or audience of in his reasoning. *Circular reasoning* is an extreme example of begging the question:

> Obviously, Saabs are for snobs because the people who drive Saabs are snobs.

Both the claim and the support say the same thing.

You can spot discourses that beg the question by looking for such words as *obviously*, *of course*, and *really*. Any defense lawyer would immediately leap up and say, "Objection!" if the prosecution were to say to the jury, "Obviously, she is guilty." The defendant's guilt or innocence is what her trial is all about. In fact, according to Anglo-Saxon law, a person is presumed innocent until proven guilty.

But even outside courts of law, a statement such as the following may well be considered begging the question:

> Of course he contributed to the senator's campaign because he is one of the people who stood to gain by the senator's election.

Certainly, the second claim does nothing to support the first; again, the statement assumes what it ostensibly set out to prove.

Personal Attacks

Another common diversion is attacking the person advancing an issue, rather than addressing the issue itself. For instance, in the course of an argument, one reasoner might say:

> This man presents a passionate argument in favor of the second amendment, yet this is the same man who was audited by the IRS last year.

If a person's trustworthiness or credibility were at all an issue in the controversy, making remarks about the character of that person might be pertinent. But most of the time—as in this case—personal attacks are diversionary tactics.

While logicians have long described personal attacks as *ad hominem* (Latin for "to the man," as opposed to an argument directed toward an issue), philosopher of rhetoric Henry Johnstone noted that all arguments are in some ways *ad hominem*. That is to say, all arguments are in some meaningful way aimed at or to particular audiences in that they are the ones who serve as judges. But fallacious arguments divert attention away from the issue and toward the character of an arguer when that is not central to the issue being argued. Chaim Perelman and Lucie Olbrechts-Tyteca call such fallacious arguments *ad personam* and define them as personal attacks that are intended to disqualify someone from reasoning regardless of the issue—like our IRS example above.

WYSIWYG

Pronounced "wizzy wig," this is an acronym for "What You See Is What You Get." WYSIWYG in this form is a product of computer-aided design. In early word-processing and design software, items looked different on the screen than after they were printed out or otherwise materialized. (Don't they still?) That's the fallacy: that context somehow does not matter and that the thing as represented on the screen could in any way *be* the thing that shows up at your doorstep, whether it be roses for your mum or a reasoning partner from Des Moines, New Mexico. "What you see is what you get" in its nonacronymic form did not originate with computer design but with sales.

False Analogy

An analogy is based on a comparison, and in reasoning by analogy, we claim that whatever we know about a familiar thing or situation we also know about another thing or situation because of the two things' similarities. *The stock market is experiencing its adolescence* is reasoning by analogy. While analogies can never prove anything conclusively, they are powerful in reasoning about things that can be otherwise.

If someone is not persuaded by an analogy you are using, he or she likely sees that the differences are more compelling than the similarities in the two things you claim are analogous. Are there more similarities or more differences between the stock market and a human being? It depends. In assessing the fallaciousness of your own and others' analogies, consider the differences as well as the similarities of the two things being compared.

Pandering

People are said to *pander* to their audiences when they use emotional appeals as diversionary tactics or scare tactics. *Pandering* means appealing to the fears and prejudices of people when those fears and prejudices are not central to the issue. Certainly, there is nothing fallacious about appealing to people's fears and values when they are central to whatever is being reasoned about. As we discussed in the brief section on pathos, the ancient rhetoricians taught that appeals to the emotions are an effective means of inducing people to do what they should do or what will benefit them. What is fallacious and unethical about pandering, however, is that it diverts people from facing issues head on and making decisions apart from their worst fears. Fund-raising organizations and insurance companies, among others, pander to audiences to get them to send or spend money. Is that an overgeneralization?

Post Hoc, Ergo Propter Hoc

As we discussed in Chapter 5, this fallacy involves mistaking chronology for causality. Just because one thing precedes another in time does not mean the first caused the second.

Faulty Use of Authority

Just because someone's claim is supported by a so-called expert does not mean that it is beyond response or rebuttal. Be particularly aware of reasoners who use only "expert testimony" to support their claims; such reasoning is often shallow and easily refuted. In fact, experts very often disagree, and careful reasoners will not only explain their reasoning before they cite authorities but also check others' sources—and, of course, their own—to make sure they are credible.

Red Herring

Yes, the red herring. The term comes from a folk-hunting custom of dragging a smelly fish across the path of fleeing prey in order to mislead the pursuing hounds. The red herring is a diversionary tactic, one nearly everyone has used at one time or another.

Speaking of my Uncle Buddy: Now *there* was a fisherman!

People are prone to resort to this fallacious tactic when they are painted into a corner in an argument with no clear way of escaping. So they try to change the subject:

> Okay, so I was less than honest in reporting my total income last year to the IRS, but doesn't everyone cheat on income taxes?

The person who uttered these words found that he could no longer deny that he had hedged in reporting his income, but unable to reasonably justify the cheating, he tried to change the subject and divert the attention from himself.

In general, you can avoid red herrings by keeping your focus on the main issue under discussion, rather than hiding in subordinate issues.

Equivocation

As we discussed in the sections on stipulative definitions, switching definitions of a word in the midst of reasoning—more briefly called *equivocation*—nearly always involves deception. *Fixed-rated* credit cards, it turns out, often do not have *fixed* rates at all; their rates may be fixed only for six months before they rise to above the prime rate.

Ancient rhetoricians pointed out that such changes of meaning can also be a form of punning—what some called *paronomasia*:

> After it rains for a week, I get as blue as the sky is on a sunny day.

You can readily recognize that the word *blue* is being used in two different senses. In less playful contexts, however, careful reasoners should make sure the terms of reasoning remain consistent during the course of reasoning.

False Dilemma

A false dilemma forces a range of choices into an *either/or* structure. In Chapter 1, we discussed the common understanding of reasoning and argument as being for or against something. The false dilemma has become one of the master fallacies of contemporary discourse. Sales and marketing techniques often attempt to get prospective targets to forget that if they choose not to buy an item or service today, they can likely return to buy it tomorrow or the day after: The choice is rarely a dilemma.

Beware of pressure tactics in any kind of reasoning that attempt to force you to choose between just two alternatives. Remember the stasis questions and the wide range of topoi that are available to you as you learn and practice the elements of reasoning.

Slippery Slope

When discussing issues that can be otherwise, reasoners who claim without support that one consequence will *inevitably* lead to a second undesirable consequence are engaging in the slippery slope fallacy. This kind of reasoning can avoid fallaciousness if it supports the links of cause and consequence with reasons that show why these things are likely to happen. But without such support, slippery slope arguments are fallacious, usually preying on people's fears of the worst:

Smoke one cigarette and you'll be hooked for life!

Well, maybe. Maybe not.

Straw Man

Another diversionary tactic, the straw man fallacy, involves exaggerating your opponent's position and then representing that exaggeration as his position. For instance, this statement

The senator would have a uranium processing plant in every town

likely exaggerates the position of the senator and sets up a false target, or straw man, that audiences will immediately reject. This kind of fallacy is also very common in advertising and political discourse. In ads, straw man fallacies center on uncool characters who are made fun of in the ads; the ads ask people to buy the product or service to avoid being as uncool as the person the ad makes fun of. In political discourse, careful reasoners will compare the claims opponents make about each other with the actual positions these individuals have shown they hold.

Scapegoating

Similar to the straw man fallacy, scapegoating is a larger phenomenon, usually involving more than single discourses or particular episodes of reasoning. Scapegoating involves blaming a difficult issue or social problem on a particular group of people. Like the names of the red herring and the straw man fallacy, the term *scapegoating* originated in a literal practice that has become a metaphor. In Leviticus, a book of laws in the Old Testament of the Bible, Aaron confessed the sins of his people over the head of a goat, and then the goat was sent into the wilderness, symbolically bearing those sins away from the people.

What does that have to do with reasoning? When a group of people is scapegoated, they are blamed collectively for the difficulty of a current situation. This is yet another diversionary tactic. After the shootings in Littleton, Colorado, news stories consistently reported that students who did not conform to certain mass cultural standards of dress or social behavior were searched, interrogated, and often detained. Political leaders sometimes blame a society's ills on one group of people, as Hitler did in the 1930s in Germany, culminating in the tragedy of the Holocaust. That is an extreme and tragic example of scapegoating.

My older brother and sisters had to take a course in high school called *Problems of Democracy.* Known as *POD,* the course introduced students to their rights and responsibilities as U.S citizens as well as to the inherent tensions and contradictions in democratic society—the relationship between the individual and the state, the possibility of tyranny of the majority, and the importance of tolerating but not ignoring dissent. While such courses are now less common than they used to be, the work of rhetoricians such as Kathleen Hall Jamieson and mass communications scholars such as Robert McChesney can help citizens learn to become more critical audiences of mass-mediated public discourse and its fallacies and diversions.

Spectator Culture, Consumer Culture, Democratic Culture

The education of the citizenry has been important to democracy for centuries. As Frederick J. Antczak discussed in his book *Thought and Character: The Rhetoric of Democratic Education* (1985), educating citizens to be able to reason together is central to democracy:

> The essential, the identifying characteristic of democracy is that here the people rule. Most obviously this means that the people are empowered to affect, in some sense to control, the future and

nature of their community. But more deeply, it means that in democracy the quality of the community and the character of its politics are determined by the quality and character of the people who constitute it. Nowhere, then, is there a more urgent need for the constant instruction and improvement of popular thought and character. Nowhere are the possibilities of education greater—nor, to be fair, are the prospects of its failure anywhere more threatening—than in democracy.

In a democracy, rhetoric as the actualizer of potential depends on citizens who are able to imagine themselves as agents of action, rather than just spectators or consumers. For most of us brought up in the second half of the twentieth century, that imagination depends, at least at first, on a kind of faith. Then, with practice, the capacity for imagining yourself as an active citizen comes from habit. Begin by reading and listening closely to the discourses around you, and then enter these public conversations—in print or on talk radio, at meetings or in classrooms—when you have something to add. With time and practice, being a citizen critic will become part of your way of life—maybe a large part, maybe a small part. Little in our culture encourages us to practice the habit of public engagement, and relatively few models are available for imitation. Choosing one from among 17 brands of deodorant or from among hundreds of styles and brands of jeans is not the same as being an active citizen in a democracy.

As Neil Postman argued in his book *Amusing Ourselves to Death: Public Discourse in an Age of Show Business* (1985), television has created a spectator culture. We live, he says, in

> a culture in which all public discourse increasingly takes the form
> of entertainment. Our politics, religion, news, athletics, education
> and commerce have been transformed into congenial adjuncts
> of show business, largely without protest or even much popular
> notice. The result is that we are a people on the verge of amusing
> ourselves to death.

Combined with the increasing emphasis on entertainment and consumption, our relative dearth of public spaces and our relative lack of experience in reasoning together in public endanger our democracy. As social critics from Christopher Lasch to Richard Sennett have observed, the twentieth century established "the lonely crowd"—people who do not find civic associations meaningful and, in fact, increasingly cannot make sense to—or even of—each other in public.

Reasoning to Invoke Citizen Critics

Given these obstacles to public discourse—and many others that we do not have time to go into here—using reasoning to actualize the potential of reasoning partners, readers, or listeners is no simple task. In order to use reasoning to get readers or listeners to imagine themselves as the kinds of people who can rise to the occasion to judge and act in ways that can make further reasoning productive, we must **invoke** as well as **address** democratic audiences.

As Michael X. Delli Carpini and Scott Keeter have argued in their book *What Americans Know about Politics, and Why It Matters* (1998), democracy, as practiced in late capitalism, is marked by "political institutions and processes designed to allow citizens to have a voice in their own governance, while at the same time limiting the impact of that voice." In addition to acquiring the habit of reasoning together—or *deliberating*—in public and making shared judgments with others, being an agent of change involves more than just addressing a preexisting audience. In addition, it involves invoking an audience that is willing to share your faith in the power of their own reasoning for negotiating difference and facilitating change.

Andrea Lunsford and Lisa Ede are rhetoricians who have been thinking and writing together for nearly 20 years about how students and other writers can best address and invoke audiences for their discourses. Lunsford and Ede explain that *audience* is so rich and complex a concept that classroom writing teachers often have to simplify it to create writing assignments that students can complete within traditional writing—and, I would add, speaking—courses. Lunsford and Ede conclude at one point that *audience* can most usefully be understood as a "complex series of obligations, needs, resources, and constraints" that both open and limit writers and speakers, readers, viewers, and listeners. Audiences are thus both textual and material—imagined and real—and they exist both inside and outside classrooms. Invoking the potential for democratic participation in audiences while addressing their current learned resistance to democratic participation highlights the need for realism and optimism together.

Historically, democracies have faced such difficulties before. Antczak's book *Thought and Character* (1985) studies nineteenth-century American rhetoric and its role in the expansion of democracy across that century. Americans have despaired for the future of their democracy before and have risen to the occasion to embrace the obligations of public education in reconstituting democratic audiences. In concluding his book, Antczak writes:

> These obligations to audience, subject, and self, these functions of adjusting ideas to people and people to ideas, define a role, a distinctive office for rhetoric in a democracy: rhetoric as central to a publicly constitutive, personally liberating education, an ever fuller identification of thought and character.

What Is a Citizen?
And a Citizen of What?

Definitions of *citizenship* have varied over time. In his book *The Good Citizen: A History of American Civic Life* (1999), Michael Schudson argues that citizenship in the United States has proceeded through four distinct eras. During the era of the founders, politics operated by the personal authority of "gentlemen" and through a politics of assent. In the nineteenth century, the development of political parties heralded a politics of affiliation. According to Schudson, mass democracy in the first three-fourths of the twentieth century "celebrated the private, rational 'informed citizen' that remains the most cherished ideal in the American voting experience today." Schudson concludes, "We require a citizenship fit for our own day."

The barrage of information we face—from television, radio, cell phones, pagers, locally and globally networked computers—arguably makes acquiring the habit of careful reasoning more and more difficult. Yet if the place of all citizens in political structures is to be maintained, our own shared reasoning is still our best hope.

The following article from the *Austin American-Statesman* (May 1999) is an example of citizen criticism that suggests how the globalization of information and of economic policy have stretched the definition of *citizen* beyond national boundaries:

Support Democracy
Susan Smith

Two years ago, I wrote about a Nigerian friend whose well-being in a nation on the verge of civil war was in question.

His friends had not heard from him in several months and our minds envisioned him in a dirty prison cell with other political detainees who were rounded up in a military crackdown on pro-democracy activists.

Today, he is well and in Texas, but he continues to fight for democracy in Nigeria through educating Americans about the need for action against a regime that has not rivaled the atrocities of Cambodia's Khmer Rouge, but is nonetheless an international monster.

June was the fourth anniversary of a military coup that nullified the 1993 election—the freest election in the country's history. The elected president languishes in prison.

Four years of human and environmental destruction have ensued: from the mysterious murder of Ken Saro-Wiwa, an environmental activist who organized against Shell Oil's pollution of Nigeria's wetlands, to Ladi Olorunyomi, a prominent woman journalist, who was recently imprisoned without being charged with a crime, according to the Africa Fund, a New York–based private organization. The fund promotes expansion of U.S. relations and investment in Africa.

In the wake of Mobutu Sese Seko's political demise and the rise of new despots in Zaire, the *New Republic* and other national magazines have questioned Africa's political future. We are part of shaping that through the policies the U.S. government adopts towards Africa's military regimes.

Nigeria does not have to become another Zaire, where the U.S. government was in bed with a dictator for decades (and on the wrong side of the people's needs) in exchange for his protection of perceived regional interests.

Recently, a bill was introduced in the U.S. House of Representatives that would ban U.S. corporate investments in Nigeria. It would affect companies such as Mobil Oil, which is the second largest producer of oil in Nigeria. (Dutch-owned Shell oil is first.) The bill is especially important because Mobil is planning a $4 billion expansion of its oil operation in Nigeria, according to the Africa Fund.

The United States is the largest customer for the oil that provides 80 percent of the Nigerian government's revenue. A blow to that pipeline through sanctions would impede the Nigerian military and help democracy advocates.

President Clinton imposed limited sanctions against Nigeria a few years ago, but none affect economic relations. Part of the reluctance to expand sanctions is because of the generous dollars Nigeria's ruling elite plow into U.S. public relations, says U.S. Rep. Maxine Waters, D-Calif. Waters is chairwoman of the Congressional Black Caucus.

"We are allowing them to advance the wrong leaders, leaders that are not about democracy, leaders that are starving people, leaders that are killing people," said Waters.

We need U.S. government policies that can help protect the lives and freedom of democracy advocates in Nigeria.

The Enthymemes of This Book

What you assert in your reasoning must be true—that is, it must be based on conjectures, definitions, causal connections, and value judgments whose validity you can vouch for and whose import you know is not merely diversionary. We can point to many claims that are not true—for instance, advertisements that attempt to persuade us if we only buy a certain product or service, we will be happier, have more friends, never feel blue (literally or figuratively?). Even worse, the twentieth century was rife with examples of leaders who quite literally misled millions of people precisely with the kinds of fallacious reasoning we outlined earlier—and with all-out lies.

If our shared public discourses cannot rise above the level of entertainment and advertising—and above the level of lies—perhaps there is no hope for us. Whether in external or internal reasoning, before we give our assent to a conclusion, we must be satisfied that the claims that led us to that conclusion are true and that the reasoning is valid. It is often very difficult to determine whether something is true. No book can give you a set of rules that will enable you to assess the truthfulness or the falsity of claims and assertions about the wide range of subjects you come across in your various roles and duties each day. In addition to education, the best guides you have are your own evolving sense of judgment and the judgments of your trusted reasoning companions. As Isocrates taught nearly 2,500 years ago: The means to good reasoning are the imitation of good reasoning, the study of good reasoning, and the practice of good reasoning.

May you practice well. Our shared future hangs in the balance. Our public discourses are what we make them.

❖ *Reasoning Practice*

1. What follows is a column I wrote for the *Daily Texan* a few years ago, after a university regent personally attacked the character of students protesting on campus. See what fallacies and diversions you can find in my reasoning in this argument. Then discuss how well this piece of reasoning stands up to your criteria for good citizen criticism.

   ### Democracy 101: A National Lesson
   Rosa Eberly

   When I picked up the *Texan* on Friday just after noon, minutes before beginning an afternoon of student advising, I could not believe what I read:

   "They're not doing themselves or anybody any good by doing what they're doing," UT System Regent Lowell Lebermann was quoted as saying.

   "We're doing everything we legally and responsibly can on the issue," he continued. "I thought our students were better informed—maybe Government 101 would be a good idea."

   Lebermann's "they" referred to the roughly 40 students who staged a sit-in all night Thursday and into Friday afternoon in order to make a point that the University is not doing everything it can to take the moral lead in public and legal arguments about affirmative action in this city, state and nation.

Perhaps Regent Lebermann had in mind Government 310, which according to the department's Web site, "Fulfills the first half of the legislative requirement for six hours of American Government." The course description says GOV 310 "provides a general background to the U.S. federal government and to the Texas state government. It emphasizes the continuing development and conflict of American and Texas government and politics."

If Government 310 teaches student-citizens that they have no right to assemble, then Regent Lebermann's suggestion is sensible; otherwise, it is what rhetoricians would call an argument *ad personam*: a fallacious claim aimed at a person's character rather than at a person's act. It represents a false deduction: that anyone who engages in direct, nonviolent protest is uneducated.

I would hope Government 310 teaches students—because most of them no longer know—that citizens' right to political participation is the foundation of democracy.

In what I have gathered over the last four years might be a Texas tradition, Lebermann maligned the character of individuals and groups who attempt to engage in direct democracy.

After Jesse Jackson brought thousands of students, faculty and staff together in prayer and deliberation over the state of affirmative action at the University last September, a *Texan* Viewpoint implied that such a rally was "shameful."

A few weeks later, in another Viewpoint, the *Texan* called student activists the following list of names: unruly, mischievous, subversive, unruly (again) and disruptive, and topped it off by suggesting that students engaging in direct democracy be expelled from the University.

Contrary to these ideologies, there is nothing "shameful" about engaging in direct democratic action. People who choose to engage in it are, necessarily, neither stupid nor in need of fundamental lessons in government.

In fact, at a time when the amount of influence an idea has on public discourse is determined by the amount of money offered by the holder of the idea, Students for Access and Opportunity and the local Anti-Racist Organizing Committee are teaching lessons in democracy, lessons we are certainly not learning from a money-and poll-driven governor's race that was declared over before it even started.

Even Regent Tony Sanchez hopped on the party line in Friday's *Texan*. He was quoted along with Lebermann: "I think it's extremely wrong to carry out your message in this way—you can't expect people to listen to you," Sanchez said.

Well, President Faulkner seemed to listen after a while. Because of last week's demonstration and sit-in, not only is the administration listening. The nation is listening. What will our message be?

2. Find a letter to the editor or an op-ed column (meaning "*opposite the ed*itorial page") in your local paper or another publication that you read regularly that you believe is an example of good citizen criticism. Your instructor will give you additional instructions for reasoning with and about what you find.

Index

Text Credits